Tales From Missouri and the Heartland

To THE MAUPIN FAMILY, I HOPE YOU ENJOY MY HEARTLAND STORIES.

Ross Malone

ROSS MALONE

author HOUSE®

AuthorHouse™
1663 Liberty Drive
Bloomington, IN 47403
www.authorhouse.com
Phone: 1-800-839-8640

First published by AuthorHouse 4/26/2010

ISBN: 978-1-4490-9717-2 (sc)
ISBN: 978-1-4490-9716-5 (hc)

Printed in the United States of America
Bloomington, Indiana

This book is printed on acid-free paper.

Forward

Missouri has been called the "Mother of the West." It's a great nickname – and very fitting. As you read the collection of stories within you may be amazed at how many people who opened the west and led to our nation's development were native Missourians.

The stories here also share some of the wisdom and humor of days gone by. Past generations have shown such a clever way with words as they level our social playing field and keep us on the right path.

I hope that this book will find its way into some Missouri History classrooms as supplemental reading. The characters were actual and factual but far more personal than the dry dates and places which sometimes make up the bulk of our textbooks. Each "tale" has a point or I wouldn't have told it. If you are a teacher using this book, please ask you students why they think each story was included. What was its main point?

Finally, the format is important. I have always felt that the greatest teachers in the world taught with stories. Aesop, Socrates, Jesus, and all the rest used stories, or fables, or parables to make their point and make it on a human level rather than the abstract. A friend recently said, "Before television, and telephone, and telegraph, there was tell-a-story." That's the way that society has used to communicate our ideas and our values for thousands of years.

I hope that you enjoy these tales and that some of them jog some pleasant or exciting memories for you. I also hope that you are a regular listener to my radio segments. If so, these stories are actually excerpted from those radio scripts. You also know that I am always searching for ideas for new tales from the heartland. If you know of an event or a person that might be interesting to others, please send a note to me at RNDMalone@att.net . Thanks!

Contents

One: The Boy Named Joyce

Joyce had a very rough childhood! The family was far from wealthy. And of course, that name. The first name Joyce was not a big help to a little boy trying to get by and avoid being picked on by the older boys.

Joyce and his brother worked at odd jobs during their elementary school years to help the family's finances. Things were bad enough and then, just when things seemed that they couldn't get worse, of course they did. Joyce heard about a job in which he could be a door-to-door salesman. He jumped at the chance and, first thing you know, he was selling perfume to the ladies of the town.

Even though he was a pretty good salesman it probably wasn't worth the price he had to pay because now he not only carried the name of Joyce but he also carried the sweet fragrances with him to school. No amount of scrubbing would completely get rid of those lingering smells on his skin and his limited wardrobe. The town bullies had all the ammunition they needed now to make his life miserable.

A big break came when Joyce found a part-time job sweeping and doing odd jobs around a drug store. He was a hard worker and his efforts were noticed and appreciated by his new employer. Traveling salesmen talked with the bright youngster and he was always interested in their stories about the larger world beyond home. Then one day a salesman came to the store with some picture postcards and a display rack. He wanted the store to display his product in exchange for a cut of the profit. The merchant agreed.

When Joyce looked at the cards he wasn't impressed. As he thought about it an idea came. Soon he was talking with his employer and running all around the area with an inexpensive camera. His artistic eye showed up in his photographs and he made sure to have them printed on the best available paper stock. Soon Joyce's picture postcards were outselling all others in his little Nebraska town.

Next he made up some cards with a Christmas theme and then some birthday cards and more. He was turning his little camera and amateur poetry into a cottage business. Soon he was asking the visiting salesmen about basic manufacturing information. They told him that Kansas City was just the place for real manufacturing.

Kansas City had plenty of hard-working people and it was a transportation hub with good highways and a network of railroads leading to every part of America. Young Joyce left to seek his fortune in the big city. Soon the quality of his product was catching on and he was busy hiring other creative people to help him turn out cards for all occasions. Some of his contributing employees were Ogden Nash, Norman Vincent Peale, Winston Churchill, Grandma Moses, and Andrew Wyeth. Of course his brothers were there working with him also. At his death in 1982 his company was valued at $1.5 Billion.

By this time you have guessed that Joyce, that hard luck kid, who persevered through everything was Joyce Hall and his famous Kansas City, Missouri location is known as Crown Center. The crown is the emblem of his famous Hallmark Cards, the Hallmark Hall of Fame, and the Hallmark Channel. The rags-to-riches story is the real life of Missourian, J. C. Hall.

Two: A Black Slave Owner

No one would ever say that John Berry Meachum's life in Kentucky was easy. He was a slave and, as a young man, his wife and child were slaves belonging to another owner. One thing in John's favor however, was that his owner taught him how to be a cooper (a barrel maker) and he allowed John to work in his spare time and earn money for himself.

In those days barrels were the most favored form of packaging for almost everything from rolled oats, to pickles, to flour. A good barrel could be stacked, rolled, and moved from place to place by one man. Demand was good and John worked hard. His barrels were known to be of good quality and one day he had saved so much money that he was able to purchase his own freedom.

His wife and child, however were still slaves and their owner announced his plans to move to St. Louis. John followed them there and found a boundless demand for barrels. In 1815 the riverfront bustled with dozens of steamboats at a time and retail commerce was booming. His skills as a cooper soon made him a lot of money and he was able to purchase the freedom of his entire family. Then he began to hire and train others as his business grew. He became a Baptist minister and started the first Black church in Missouri.

At this time John made a controversial decision. He decided to start purchasing slaves to work in his cooperage and on his riverboats. For this, some people condemn him without any other consideration.

There is another side to this story however. The slaves who were purchased by John were promised freedom just as soon as they would meet two conditions. They had to have a rudimentary education so people couldn't easily cheat them, and they must have a skill which could support them and their eventual families. No one knows how many slaves John Berry Meachum bought and freed over the next several years but the number was large.

One day John purchased an old steamboat and repaired it. This was the beginning of a new enterprise and new skills and trades for many more people. Then one day an old riverboat became the symbol of John's winning attitude.

He had started a school for black children but, at that time, even free blacks were not allowed to be educated. For a time the officials looked the other way but were finally forced to enforce the law. They closed John's little school. John had never been one to take "no" for an answer and he wasn't about to start now. He told the students to meet him on the riverfront where they boarded a waiting steamboat and sailed out past the middle of the river. Now that they were legally in Illinois, classes could begin.

John Berry Meachum was a man who went from dire poverty to the owner of prosperous businesses and a steamboat line. He was able to free himself and many others from the clutches of slavery. Yet, he as a former slave, is sternly criticized for owning slaves himself. It's easy to see both sides of this argument. What do you think?

Three: The Golden Rule Merchant

The Irish built the railroads connecting east and west across Missouri. They left terrible persecution at the hands of the British in Ireland. There they had been allowed to own nothing larger than a goat and now they had arrived in a place where good land was cheap and sometimes even given away in land rushes. From the rocky soil of the Old Sod they found themselves on a North American prairie where the soil was so deep that no plow, no matter how deep, could find rocks.

After the tracks were laid and the trains were running the railroad companies sold the land along the route to anyone with the money to make the purchase. These Irish had been sheltered and fed as they progressed across the state so their wages were mostly intact. They purchased this prairie land, continued to work hard, and prospered.

James's family was among those hard-working honest people who built the railroads and then stayed on to farm and become the railroad's first and best customers. Deeply religious and ethical, James' father taught his family to always live by the Golden Rule.

While still a very young man James believed that it was a sign from Heaven when he was offered a position in the Golden Rule Store in Wyoming. He moved into the attic and gave his all to managing the store into prosperity. Within five years he had saved enough money to buy out the partners and this became the first of many "dry goods" stores which he would own.

At this time in the early 1900s it was customary to "haggle" on almost every sale. James declared that his stores would offer "One Price for All" and set all prices so he could earn a fair profit on each item and no more. The Golden Rule was the unofficial motto at all his stores. He had a profit sharing plan for his managers and he promoted from within. He was quoted as saying, "Give me a stock clerk with a goal and I'll give you a man who'll make history. Give me a man with no goals and I'll give you a stock clerk."

By 1927 the dry goods store in James' home town of Hamilton, Missouri was up for sale and he bought it making it his 500th store. He was well on his way to being the nation's second largest retailer. During the 1930s he was hit hard by the Great Depression so he borrowed against his own life insurance policies in order to meet the company payroll. He truly lived the Golden Rule.

Multimillionaire James remained a common man at heart and rode the city busses to his office in New York City. He enjoyed visiting all of his stores and would sometimes quietly step behind the counters to wait on unsuspecting customers. His biggest joy came when he frequently returned to his farm next to the railroad at Nettleton, near Hamilton Missouri.

There he would get comfortable in overalls and drive his old Chevy coupe around the countryside to visit with neighbors.

Old timers who remember him are quick to say that he really was a man who lived by the Golden Rule. By now you have probably figured out that this good man's name was James Cash Penney. J. C. Penney to his friends.

Four: The Boy on the Coin

Many of our famous and noteworthy Midwesterners were born farther east and then came west to the heartland. This was especially true in the very early days of our country. One however, began his life way out west near the Rocky Mountains and then came east for the benefits of civilization in the little river town of St. Louis.

We English speakers might call him John but that would just be an approximation of his given name. John was born to his mother who was a slave in the Hidatsa Indian village until his father won her in a game of bones (dice). As a boy he was so bossy that one American soldier called him "Pompey" after Pompeii, the Roman General. This army officer loved the bossy little general and would come to play an important part in the boys life.

Destined for a life of high adventure, by the time he was a year old he had already traveled from the Great Plains to the Pacific Ocean. This fact caused him to be the only child ever depicted on a United States coin. The officer saw something special in this boy and offered to let him live in St. Louis with his very own family and to attend school for all the benefits which an education can bring. At 4 ½ years of age his mother took him to St. Louis and to the education which was offered. They found a new American city with many French and Spanish influences everywhere they turned. It must have been so exciting!

The officer was now a General of the Army and this boy's new life must have seemed very wonderful and strange. However, this was the time when the boy first encountered the prejudice which would follow him because of his mother's ancestry. The General's wife would not permit John to live and grow up with her children. Trying to keep his promise, the General sent John to live in a boarding house and paid for the best education available.

John came to St. Louis speaking two Indian languages and French. His school was taught in English and many St. Louisans still spoke Spanish. Like his mother, he had a gift for languages.

At 19 John left St. Louis and headed back west into the land away from the bustle of the city and took a job in a trading post near the present day Kansas City. There he met a naturalist, Paul Wilhelm, the Duke of Württemberg, Germany. The Duke was amazed at the level of education of this young man and at his ability with languages. A great friendship had begun. By now you have figured out what the Duke had discovered – that John was really Jean Baptiste Charbonneau, the son of Sacagawea and Toussaint Charbonneau. The General in St. Louis was the explorer, William Clark.

Young Charbonneau eventually left the United States and sailed for Europe with the Duke. He was embraced by the Dukes friends all over Europe and learned much while he was there. Travels in Europe were followed by adventures in Africa and then, in 1829, the two friends traveled to the Caribbean and then onward to St. Louis.

Now with an educational and experiential background like no other, he decided to go west once again. He joined John Jacob Astor's American Fur Company and became a mountain man like his father. Through most of the rest of his life he shared adventures with men like John Colter, Kit Carson, Jim Bridger, James Beckweth, and John C. Fremont. His final years were a mixture of adventures along the Mexican Border and a peaceful time working anonymously as a hotel clerk in northern California. In 1866 he decided to have one last adventure and he headed north into the Oregon Territory where he died at a stagecoach stop. Sacagawea is famous for her adventure but most Americans aren't even aware of her son who may have had more adventures than any other person since Marco Polo. And Jean Baptiste Charbonneau was the baby on the Sacajawea dollar, the only child on American money.

Five: Auguste Chouteau

Pierre Laclede was a forward-looking and intuitive businessman in New Orleans. He could recognize an opportunity when he saw it. This time the opportunity was in the un-charted Louisiana Territory. Up there, somewhere in that distant land, the two largest rivers on the continent met. One of them, the Missouri, flowed all the way from a great mountain range. Two other large rivers met the Mississippi River near this juncture. It was all un-mapped and vague but it seemed a great place for a trading post and maybe even a city.

Getting upstream on that powerful Mississippi River was no easy task and only the sturdiest of men would or could even attempt it. Arriving at the confluence of the rivers would call for a flurry of clearing the land, building a fortress, coming to terms with the Indians, and doing all of the other things necessary for establishing a settlement. Only the roughest and toughest of men could be selected and it would take someone very special to command the respect and the efforts of this band.

Laclede's choice for this job was his nephew, Auguste Chouteau. Many must have wondered about his choice but Laclede recognized something that many others didn't. No one really knows how eagerly or reluctantly Chouteau accepted the job but in 1763 he did accept the challenge and set off into the wilderness.

Arriving at the confluence of the rivers, Laclede realized that it was not possible to establish anything there. It was low land and it obviously flooded frequently. He took the party back downstream to where he remembered seeing some hills and mounds above the western bank of the Mississippi. This, he decided, would be the spot.

Under his direction, work began and a fort was built. Chouteau named the place in honor of an ancient King of France, St. Louis. Soon word spread among the mountain men that a trading post was available and word spread among the settlements in Louisiana that a safe haven was now there for them in the middle of the continent. The place grew faster than anyone could have predicted and soon Uncle Laclede arrived and built his beautiful home with walnut interiors and crystal chandeliers. When Lewis and Clark arrived to prepare for their expedition, Laclede and Chouteau were their biggest supporters. As Lewis and Clark made their way westward, they named many of our western rivers and mountains in honor of Laclede and Chouteau. When Sacajawea brought her son to St. Louis, Chouteau adopted him as his Godson.

Now, you may have known much or all of this but how about this one final fact? When Auguste Chouteau left home in charge of that rough and tough group of explorers, hunters, builders, and frontiersmen, he managed to earn their respect with his intelligence, judgment, hard work, and maturity even though he was only 13 years old!

Six: The Shepherd of the Hills

The most widely sold book in the world is the Bible. For many years the second most widely sold book was a story of the Missouri Ozarks. Its author, Harold Bell Wright, was a small town preacher with a huge talent for finding and writing a compelling story. For those with an interest in Missouri history, The Calling of Dan Matthews presents a wonderful look at the life in that typical town during the first decade of the 1900s.

The Rev. Mr. Wright was the minister of the First Christian Church in Lebanon, Missouri and might have seemed a perfectly normal part of that Bible Belt community. There was something very different about him however. He noticed the drama in the lives of people around him and in the broader communities during a troubled time.

Though he wrote 18 other books too, his masterpiece was the story of some ordinary people trying to get by in the hills and hollows around Branson. As with people in any community, there were the pretty young women, the hot-headed and mis-understood young men, the suspicious and un-welcoming established families, and in this story there was someone else. A wise old man, seemingly new to the Ozarks whose mysterious past helped him to understand the many people he encountered here.

An Ozarks version of the KKK also figures into this story. Groups like the KKK who operated outside the law had to do so in secret so they would often choose a hilltop for their meetings. This would be even better if the hill (the knob) were clear of trees. In other words, if it were bald. That is how these merchants of fear and hate came to be known as Baldknobbers.

In addition to selling so many books, this story continues to be performed in the Branson area on a daily basis and it has been made into no less than five movies! The best known of these movies features a young John Wayne and it can still be seen from time to time on cable TV. Wright is said to have been the first author to sell a million books and the first author to earn a million dollars from his writing.

President Ronald Reagan loved the writing of Harold Bell Wright and told his family that a traveling printer in one book (The Printer of Udell) had been an inspiration and a role model to Mr. Reagan in his early Christian life. Wright's books were always full of "country values" such as hard work, honesty, responsibility, and integrity. One author pointed out that Wright's heroes were never the person with the fastest gun but the one with the strongest character.

By now I'll bet you've figured out that Harold Bell Wright's classic story is <u>The Shepherd of the Hills</u>. But have you read it or seen it performed? The next time you see it on the TV schedule or the next time you drive past Shepherd of the Hills Theater in Branson, plan to stop and spend an evening with the wonderful characters. The theater has produced this show for over forty years non-stop. Hey, Broadway, how's that for a long-running show?

Seven: President Hiram

Hiram was born in 1822 at Point Pleasant, Ohio, the oldest of six children. He was a good student and caught the eye of many during his school years. One congressman in particular noticed Hiram and nominated him to attend the US Military Academy at West Point. While at that school he made friends with a young man from St. Louis and through him met his sister, Julia Dent. In 1848 Hiram married this daughter of the prosperous Missouri family. Her parents gave them a gift of 80 acres of farm land and this brought Hiram to live in Missouri.

On this new land he built a large two-story dog trot style cabin with glass windows and a cedar shingled roof. Hiram did much of the work himself but many friends helped and the new home was completed in only three days. They named the place Hardscrabble and the name fit. He found himself trying to make ends meet by doing the most menial of tasks and would often shovel wagonloads of gravel from a nearby stream and haul the gravel to sell for construction in St. Louis. After a short time they moved to the home of Julia's family because her father had died and Hiram set to the business of managing his farm and the Dent farm. Once again, this did not go well.

When he was 38 has father bought a store in Illinois and the family moved there. Hiram and Julia tagged along. Hiram was hired to work in the store which his father owned and his younger brother managed. He spent much time "Traveling through the northwest..." which in those days meant little towns in Wisconsin, Minnesota, and Iowa. No matter what he tried to do he couldn't seem to succeed at anything. The only time in his life when he seemed really good at anything was during his few years as an army officer.

Then, in 1861, the Civil War broke out and Hiram re-enlisted. Soon his military brilliance began to show and was even brought to the attention of President Lincoln, his Commander-In-Chief. Lincoln promoted him to Lt. General and named him to command all Union forces for the remainder of the war. When the war ended, this hero was swept into the office of President of the United States.

If you don't remember the president named Hiram – well, that's part of the story too. When that congressman appointed him to West Point he wasn't really sure of Hiram's actual name. He guessed wrongly and listed Hiram Ulysses Grant as Ulysses S. Grant. Hiram not only didn't mind, he liked being called U.S. Grant and he just kept that name.

I suppose that we would have to say that, as President, Grant wasn't very successful either. It seems that he trusted people who weren't worthy of that trust. They scandalized the capital and everything they did reflected on the president who had appointed them. His reputation and his fortune fell. In his last years he was destitute and in desperate need of help. Another Missourian came to his rescue. Samuel Clemens, a.k.a. Mark Twain. He helped Grant to publish a wonderful two-volume set of his memoirs and then traveled the country with Grant basically showing him how to conduct a book tour and sell the product. It was enough that Grant and Julia could live out their lives in relative comfort and dignity.

The next time you're in beautiful Galena, Illinois or visiting the Clydesdales at Anheuser Busch's Grant's Farm in St. Louis, remember this man who struggled at everything but found his place in history as one of our greatest generals.

Eight: John Colter

Have you ever heard of Colter's Hell? Of course you have but maybe not by that name. After all Colter's Hell doesn't sound like a place you would want to take your family on a vacation but when John Colter told people about it, they didn't even believe that such a place could exist.

John Colter was born to be an explorer. As a young man he spent as much time in the woods as possible. Though young, he was already recognized in the Kentucky country as an especially good hunter. This is where Meriwether Lewis found him and invited him to join the Corps of Discovery. John Colter earned his living with the expedition by walking the riverbanks and hunting for the other members who were manning the boats. With over 40 men, each working so hard that they required six pounds of meat each day to keep their strength, Colter had a monumental task.

Though he was one of the youngest, he was soon recognized as one of the brightest and most valuable members of the expedition and earned some leadership responsibilities as the expedition progressed. On the homeward journey, he was granted an early discharge so he could do more exploring and trapping in the wild mountains of the west.

In 1809 Colter had joined with former expedition member, John Potts, and was hunting and trapping for Manuel Lisa's expedition. At this time he and Potts were captured by the very territorial Blackfoot and sentenced to death. It was decided that Potts and Colter should be turned loose naked and barefoot to be hunted down for sport. They separated and ran and stumbled over the stones and prickly pear cactus leaving a trail of blood for their pursuers. Eventually Potts was captured and slain. Colter managed to hide in some floating debris (possibly a beaver dam) in the river.

Colter returned to Missouri and settled on a spot which he had seen in 1804 overlooking the Missouri River near present day New Haven, Missouri. He married an Indian woman and they prospered, leaving a large family which still gathers in New Haven to honor his memory. He served in the War of 1812 with his friend and neighbor, Nathan Boone. It was Daniel's son, Nathan who purchased a tombstone for Colter when he died while enlisted in Boone's company.

Oh, yes. That part about Colter's Hell. Well it seems that when Captain William Clark was preparing his journals for submission to President Jefferson, It was Colter who had to fill in the details about a place where steam, smoke and sulfurous fumes come shooting out of the ground. A place where the ground shook beneath your feet and the earth had turned all sorts of strange colors. Many didn't even believe that such a place really existed. Those who did called it Colter's Hell.

Yes, John Colter had been the first white man to discover what would later become the world's first national park. It would also be given it's original Indian name, Yellowstone.

Nine: The Greatest Earthquake

When Americans think of earthquakes we usually think about San Francisco or Alaska. Of course we know that the Middle East is riddled with fault lines and earthquakes often devastate that area. The biggest earthquake in our country's history, however, was a strange happening centered around New Madrid in Missouri.

Strange is a good description for several reasons. First, It was not just one quake but a series of more than 2000 shocks spread over a period of 2 years. Second, the size of the tremors was strange. The first was an 8.0 on the Richter Scale. That would make it 10 times more powerful than the one which destroyed San Francisco. Then there were two more 8.0s in fairly rapid succession.

Small quakes continued for about a year and then an even larger quake hit the same region. Then after another year of small quakes, the largest shock of all hit that part of Missouri. To repeat, in what is now called "the" New Madrid earthquake, there were five gigantic earthquakes interspersed with more than 2000 minor quakes!

Another strange feature of this event was the "sandblows." Here fountains of sand were forced up from deep underground and blown into the air. The remains of these geysers of sand can still be seen on the landscape.

We've all heard the stories that the ground shook so violently that church bells rang on the east coast. Other events were just as shocking. A small group of hunters were on the shore of a lake in southeast Missouri when the ground swelled up in front of them. While they watched, the water drained away and the lake disappeared. On the other side of the Mississippi, the land began to sink and water from the river began to flood in. The result can be visited today. It's known as Reelfoot Lake.

We have all heard that the water in the Mississippi ran backwards. Three huge ridges of the earth did rise up and block the river and it did indeed run backwards. What is just as interesting is that, when it began to flow south again, the river took a new course. This is why Kaskaskia, Illinois is now on the Missouri side of the River.

There were two things about that time which amounted to good fortune for the inhabitants. One is that the homes of both Indians and settlers were constructed of wood. Wood is relatively pliable and the damage was not so severe as if there had been brick construction. These homes were also very small. The other fortunate fact is that just not many people lived in the area at that time.

When this happens again, we can only guess what affect there will be on giant population centers such as St. Louis and Memphis or even what will happen to the thousands of nice brick homes, colleges, malls, highways, bridges, and other structures which stretch from Cape Girardeau to the south. Do you know what to do if your home begins to shake?

Ten: The Honey War

Did you know that there have been actual border wars between some of our own Heartland states? Sometimes silly and sometimes tragic they certainly did happen. In the early days of Missouri the northern border was determined to be a line stretching due west from the "rapids of the River Des Moines." Confusion developed as no one could find any rapids on the Des Moines River. Just north of the river's juncture with the Mississippi is a swift-moving area of the Mississippi River which was called the "Des Moines Rapids" and this is probably what the cartographers and politicians had in mind.

The area south of that line was deemed to be Missouri and to the north was the Wisconsin Territory. Later of course the southern part of Wisconsin would be sectioned off and called Iowa. Different surveyors were hired and they produced four different parallel borders. The sheriffs of the bordering counties had a great deal of trouble enforcing any laws and collecting taxes was out of the question.

One settler of The Strip as they called it was Samuel Riggs. He was the sheriff of Davis County, Iowa. His cousin, Jonathan Riggs, was the sheriff of neighboring Schuyler County, Missouri. Jonathan arrested Samuel for infringing on the laws of Missouri and Samuel then arrested Jonathan for holding office in Missouri while living in Iowa. He kept Jonathan in jail for two months.

Matters came to a head in 1839 when an unknown farmer from Missouri cut three bee trees in The Strip. The honey was valuable as a sweetener and the beeswax was used to make the finest candles so this was a matter of some importance on the frontier. The new Iowa Territory tried the man, even though he wasn't present, and fined him $1.50. Naturally this inflamed the Missourians and they called out their motley militia. Iowa then for the very first time called out their militia to meet the challenge. Thus, the event has gone down in history as the "Honey War."

By December, 3,600 ragtag militiamen were gathered along the vague border. The Iowans with only 1200 men had four generals, as well as 132 other officers including one lieutenant with a beautiful uniform which was the most admired thing on the field. Everyone else was wearing their work clothes.

The Missourians were armed with a great variety of weapons including one man who planned to use a sausage stuffer. I'm not sure what it would be like to be attacked with a sausage stuffer. The Lewis County, Missouri Militia bivouacked in the cold and snow for two nights even though they hadn't brought enough blankets and no tents at all. They did however have their priorities in line because they remembered to bring five wagons of whiskey.

The war probably ended with the men returning home with tales of great bravery and daring. However there were no deaths, no injuries, and no shots fired from either side. It must be said that the Iowans were the most aggressive because at one point, many of them were chanting, "Death to the Pukes." But, even with such atrocities, the Honey War was over and Missouri and Iowa have been good neighbors ever since.

Eleven: The Original Tom Boy

Martha was born in 1852 in pleasant little Princeton, Missouri on our northern prairie. She was the oldest of six children and by age 15 her parents had both died of natural causes. This left the teenager as head of the family.

Martha was described as "extremely attractive" and as a "pretty, dark-eyed girl" but she wasn't the frilly feminine type. She was an excellent shot and loved to spend most of her time with the men on hunting trips. While still very young she went west with her family to the Wyoming territory. She loved the adventure of this trip.

She worked as a dishwasher, waitress, dance hall girl, nurse, and an ox team driver. Then in 1870 she put on the uniform of a soldier and began her work as an army scout. Soon she discovered that men's clothing better suited her rough lifestyle and she dressed as a man from then on. At one time she was asked to deliver important dispatches from General Crook and she swam the Platte River and traveled 90 miles at top speed while wet and cold. It made her very ill but few men and fewer women could have done such a feat.

In 1876 she was in Deadwood, South Dakota where she met Wild Bill Hickok. He had just left Missouri after a shootout on the square in Springfield. Martha became infatuated with him but he didn't share her feelings. Martha pursued him until he was shot to death during a card game that same year. She claimed that she went after the shooter with a meat cleaver because she was so agitated that she left her gun at home. According to her, the only thing that kept her from revenge was that the shooter was hanged before she could get to him.

In 1881 she was running an inn near Yellowstone Park when she met and married a Texan, Clinton Burke. They moved to Boulder where she tried again to run a business but was not very successful.

Then in 1893 Martha decided to take a "regular" job. She began appearing in Buffalo Bill's Wild West Show. She became one of his most famous characters as a sure shot and trick rider. In 1893 she died at the age of 51 and was buried next to Wild Bill Hickok.

Now maybe you have figured out just who Martha really was. Her full name was Martha Jane Cannary. This rough & tough beauty once told some admiring soldiers that to pester her was to "court calamity." From this, the Missouri-born heroin of the west was known to all as "Calamity Jane."

Twelve: Place Names

You've probably wondered just how some cities and towns across the Heartland got such unique names. In fact some names are pretty peculiar – such as the Kansas City suburb named Peculiar. There are two stories about how this place got its name. The most likely is that the postmaster of the un-named neighborhood grew frustrated trying to give the place a name which wasn't already in use somewhere else. The Post Office Department reportedly told him to try something new or peculiar, so he did!

Many places got their names as little communities were wanting to get started and to identify with important places and events in the world. That's how Missouri ended up with such places as Japan, Cuba, Mexico, and Paris. Others are named after heroes. These would include Rolla, Missouri and Rolla Kansas. The funny thing about these places is that the original settlers wanted to honor a hero, Sir Walter Raleigh but they didn't know how to spell his name so they took their best shot – and missed by a mile.

Other towns named for heroes include Boonville, Laclede, Franklin, Hannibal, or Jefferson. Counties were also named for heroes. In fact Andrew Jackson was such a hero that two counties were named for him. Can you think of which ones they might be? No, Andrew County is not one of them. It was named for Andrew Jackson Davis. Lewis and Clark along with Boone and Callaway, and Washington, Jefferson, and Franklin were all named for heroes.

Many Missouri towns were named after places farther east. This especially shows in the areas where Daniel Boone and his friends settled on the north side of the Missouri River.

The devil had a special place in the hearts of early Missourians. In his honor they named at least eight places including Devil's Elbow a small community in Butler County. This place earned its name as lumberjacks would try to raft logs down the Big Piney River and always had trouble with a sharp swift turn in the river. Early travelers noted a place in Franklin County which they named the Devil's Race Ground. This large whirlpool by St. Albans is now gone and replaced with an Island. Missouri's devil seems to be a clean one because he has given us names like Devil's Wash Basin, Devil's Washboard, and the Devil's Washpan.

Many Missouri places are named Osage. This includes a town, a river and a county. Early explorers called the Osage the Huzzah or the Hoozaw and these names too are found around our state. Neosho and Nixa (Niska) are also Native American names. Nodaway is an Indian word meaning "quiet waters." Pemiscot means "liquid mud" and Meramec means "catfish" in the native language. Gasconade is said to have meant "snakes with white mouths open." That paints a good picture of the Gasconade River! My home town used to be named Wyota which was the name of the original Osage village there. I think we lost something by changing the name.

Finally, I'll bet you thought I forgot. Those two Missouri counties named for Andrew Jackson. One of course is Jackson County which contains Kansas City. The name, Andrew, had already been taken but the folks in this west central Missouri county really wanted to honor the president known as "Old Hickory" so they decided to name their home Hickory County.

Thirteen: Orphan Trains

In the late 1800s and early 1900s the United States had a terrible social problem. Orphan Children crowded the streets of all the big eastern cities. Each child had his or her own story of becoming parentless but each had found themselves in an orphanage which was overflowing and unable to properly care for the children. A solution was offered in which the children would be sent by train to the Midwest where good farm families might have need for help and could offer more of a home than the orphanage could ever be. 100,000 came to Missouri!

They were given sandwiches and apples and put on the train with one adult chaperone. They slept sitting upright in their seats. At each little whistle stop town, they would be taken off the train and lined up at the local opera house or community center. From this lineup, the Midwesterners would select the children they wanted. This was not always the happy beginning of a new life. Many children, having already lost their parents, were now separated from their brothers and sisters for the first time. Those not selected were loaded back onto the train and hauled to the next town for the next lineup. A sample announcement is shown on the next page.

Wanted
Homes for Children
A company of homeless children from the East
will arrive at
TROY, MO., ON FRIDAY, FEB.25, 1910

These children are of various ages and of both sexes, having been thrown friendless upon the world. They come under the auspices of the Children's Aid Society of New York. They are well disciplined, having come from the various orphanages. The citizens of This community are asked to assist the agent in finding good homes recommended by the local committee. They must treat the children In every way as a member of the family, sending them to school, church, Sabbath school and properly clothe them until they are 17 years old. The following well-known citizens have agreed to act as local committee to aid the agents in securing homes.

O.H. AVERY, E.B.WOOLFOLK, H.F. CHILDERS
WM.YOUNG, G.W. COLBERT

Applications must be made to, and endorsed by, the local committee. An address will be made by the agent. Come and see the children and hear the address. Distribution will take place at the
Opera House, Friday, Feb. 25, at 1:30 P.M.

As sad as this all seems, it was the new beginning for anywhere from 150,000 to 400,00 children whose only hope for a better life was a tearful trip to the Heartland.

Fourteen: Hannah Cole

In the earliest days of settlement west of St. Louis there were many little groups of pioneers who made their way up the various rivers and settled in clusters where they could support each other as they developed the rich river bottom land. The Cole family, along with two other families of close relatives, were in the process of emigrating to this newly opened territory just after the Louisiana Purchase. Then, in 1810, near where Hermann, Missouri is now, disaster struck.

The pioneers were camped on an island in the middle of the river for safety from the surrounding Indians. Their fears were well-founded but their defenses were not enough and a night-time attack cost the group seven invaluable horses. The Cole brothers and others chased the Pottawatomies and, in the fight which followed, Hannah's brother-in-law received 26 wounds but made it back to camp. Her husband was not so fortunate. In this situation with no one to defend the women and children and no men to clear the new land and farm it, the only sensible thing was to return to St. Louis or St. Charles and hope to get by in whatever way possible.

Hannah Cole made the courageous decision to continue on upstream and look for the type of place that they came seeking. She stopped and stayed with another group of pioneers on the north side of the river where in 1816 they would lay out the little town of Franklin but for now they were just camping and trying to stay alive long enough to get a start. Some, like Hannah, felt that they should relocate across the river and build their new town on the bluffs but most enjoyed the easy access to the river and the boats which were now using it in increasing numbers. Flooding was a worry but, so far, everything was fine.

In January, 1810 Hannah Cole moved across the river and built a cabin on the bluff where Bonnville stands now. She and her children almost starved that winter. They reported having only acorn, slippery elm bark, and one wild turkey. The folks in Franklin thought those on the bluff were silly for giving up such easy assess to the benefits of the river but, sure enough, rivers do flood and the new little town was swept away. Hannah's cabin was soon enlarged and took the name Cole's Fort. Now this lady who had lost everything was the one to whom others looked for their security. Her cabin became the first church in the area as well as the first schoolhouse.

Before the flooding of Franklin, Hannah's sons operated a ferry across the river between the towns. Soon Hannah was selling land and home sites to newcomers and then a stagecoach began using Bonnville as the starting point for a southern route reaching settlers who were homesteading away from the river. Hannah Cole, more than anyone else had provided the security then the entrepreneurial drive to develop the central part of the state.

When it was time to move the capital city from St. Charles to a more central part of the state, the constitution declared that it should be near the juncture of the Missouri and the Osage Rivers. This was for reasons of transportation, communication, and settlement on these two large rivers.

Hannah Cole would have enjoyed the fact that the new capital would be near her home. She would have appreciated the fact that the new city was situated atop some bluffs overlooking the river. And how honored must she have felt to know that the new capital city of her state would be located in – Cole County!

Rocky Ridge Ranch
Mansfield, Missouri

Fifteen: The Lady From Rocky Ridge

Her father was probably one of those A.D.D. boys. He couldn't stay still. He always had too much energy and had to be on the move. Fortunately for him, he lived in a time when such a young man could move from place to place, build up a farm and a homestead and then sell it for a profit. Her mother did not share the father's love for change. In her view, every time they got their home all fixed up and comfortable, it was time to move west.

I'm sure she understood her mother's feelings but she shared some of her father's love of adventure. She loved the opportunities to meet Indian children, to encounter wolves on the moonpath of a frozen lake, and even learned to love the big-hearted though rascally men who inhabited the frontier.

One of my favorite stories from her childhood tells of a time when a cow fell through the roof of her family's sod home and dangled its legs through and into the house. When they finally got the cow free it left a huge hole in the roof. Many young girls would have complained and dwelled on how miserable their life was when they didn't even have a solid roof over their heads. This girl however, looked up from her bed and was thrilled to see thousands of stars. She felt that she had the best ceiling of all. She epitomized optimism. She was definitely a "glass half full" person!

When she married, she and her husband began to look for a place where they could settle for life. No more moving around. Soon they discovered a spot just east of Mansfield, Missouri and knew it was home. They named the place Rocky Ridge Ranch and set to building a home. It's hard to imagine how she crawled on the steep roof in her long dress and petticoats to nail cedar shake shingles to the roof. Dangerous? Yes but she did it.

It was a stroke of luck when she found a job at the library in Mansfield where she could be surrounded by lots of people including children and lots of books. She loved those very things. At the story times she would often tell the children about her adventures on the frontier whether it was in the forests of Minnesota or the dry prairies of eastern Kansas. The children weren't the only ones enthralled by the adventures and the humor of her tales.

Her coworkers there in Mansfield encouraged her to submit some of her stories to magazines. The magazines published them and the public went wild. The editors were soon clambering for more.

By now you have figured out that this woman who wrote of all her experiences in all those little houses was Laura Ingalls Wilder. Her last books were about her life there on the Rocky Ridge. Of course her stories were published in many languages and are still extremely popular today. Her experiences still have meaning to reach across generations and the television series based on her books has been in reruns for decades. Laura Ingalls Wilder is truly a symbol of the Heartland.

Sixteen: Bees

Have you heard of bees? I don't mean the insects. I mean the gatherings. Old timers in Missouri would often gather together and help each other in times of need. Of course reciprocation was always expected. Quilts could be made at quilting bees, husking bees could get the corn harvest ready, and road bees could allow everyone to benefit from having a new or improved road. You could call a bee for almost any need. Bees were always famous for contests, good food, and fun.

Closely related to bees were raisings. The men would gather to raise barns for neighbors, raise a house for newlyweds, or raise a new church for their religious community. At all of the bees and raisings, the entire family would come. For children on the frontier it was a rare opportunity to play with children outside their own family. For young men and women it was an opportunity to be noticed. For the elders, it was a chance to get to know their neighbors and to make the community a better place.

Camp meetings and brush arbor meetings were also important parts of frontier lives. At a camp meeting the attendees would bring their tents and stay for several days at a time. They could count on some good Bible-thumping preachers, some wonderful gospel singing with string musicians accompanying, and all sorts of good food. One of the main aspects of these events was the social part because here you got to meet neighbors from near and far. Sometimes thousands of people would sit on logs and listen to the best of the preachers or join in the best of the hymns.

Brush arbor meetings were similar in many ways. They were usually done in places where there was no church building. Trees would be bent over and tied together and then cut brush would be thrown on top and a long shady sort of tunnel would be formed to let in the breeze but not the sun.

Many Missourians still remember Pie Suppers and Boxed Dinner events. Here the men and boys could bid on pies, lunch, and other goodies secretly brought in by the women and girls. When the man or boy bought a pie at auction he bought the right to sit and share it with its maker. This was a common way to raise money for operating country schools.

Even today men around the state enjoy turkey shoots but this contest of skill and luck has been around for a long time. Missouri's great artist, George Caleb Bingham, immortalized a similar event in his painting, "Shooting for the Beef." The contest he depicted was definitely a matter of skill and the prize was a steer. The contest was not only a chance to provide enough beef for your family but to meet with the other men and collect some "braggin' rights."

The common thread among all of these events is that they were creative and inventive ways for early settlers and some more recent to have a good time while doing something important for their neighbors and the good of the community.

Seventeen: Natives of the Heartland

There are many things around us even today which bear witness to the original Americans who lived here before us. Near St. Louis there are the mounds which were built up during hundreds of years of occupation by the folks we now call the Mound Builders. St. Louis itself used to be called Mound City and there are still many things in St. Louis which carry that name. Those particular mounds have all given way to bulldozers in what some call progress. Wouldn't it be nice if they had saved some and incorporated them in greenspace?

Just north of St. Louis near Alton is the great Piassa Bird. This dragon-like creature has stared down from its bluff since recorded history and probably much longer.

Of course arrowheads and other stone tools can still be found if you have eyes sharp enough for the hunt. I, along with several other boys, once found an entire cave full of Indian treasures in a bluff above the Niangua River. I'm sure there are others waiting to be discovered.

One of my favorite sights from days gone by is what I call Indian Trees. Many people have other names for them. No one is sure just why the trees were formed in the way that they are and there are probably several reasons. As a sapling, a tree would be bent over and tied to point in a particular direction. It seems that sometimes they pointed toward a good source of fresh water. Others seem to point toward a cave or some other place where food might be safely stored. For whatever reason, these trees were bent and then grew pointing earthward. Of course trees are phototropic and tend to grow upward toward the light. Just beyond the point where they were tied they did indeed turn upward and some stand there today having grown up, then over sharply to one side, then upward again. This very distinctive shape marks something significant from a time beyond our knowledge. Of course any of these trees still in existence would be well over a hundred years old.

Some the best things the Indians have left us include tomatoes, potatoes, corn, popcorn, pumpkins, many kinds of squash, and other good foods. It's hard to imagine life without things like potatoes and corn.

The next time you get a chance, take a look at our map and see how many places around here still carry their Indian names.

| Missouri = land of the big canoes | Meramec = catfish |
| Huzzah = the Osage people | Gasconade = snakes with white mouths open |

There are cities like Kansas City, Neosho, and Osceola named for particular Indian tribes or nations. Then there are the Indian names which were long ago recorded in French then translated into English. Through the translations we have lost the meanings of words like Ozarks, Taum Sauk Mountain and more. By our arrogance and not paying closer attention to the Indians, I wonder what else we have lost.

Eighteen: Early Elections

You stop at the neighborhood store to pick up a bottle of wine for dinner. The wine, beer, and liquors are all roped off and not for sale. Oh, sure you think. It's Election Day. No one can buy or sell alcoholic beverages while the poles are open. What's that about?

In Missouri's early days the elections were viewed as vitally important and voting was one of the most earnest endeavors of a man's life. But it was very different than what we see today. I want you to look at he front of this book to see one of George Caleb Bingham's most famous paintings about early Missouri. It's titled <u>The County Election</u> and it pictures Election Day activities in Arrow Rock, Missouri.

In this painting the men are wearing their Sunday best and lined up for the opportunity to cast their ballots. A great deal of discussion is going on in the line. At one end of the line people are taking the oath in preparation for balloting. At the beginning of the line a table is set up in the street with jugs of whiskey and many are imbibing. Some political operatives were in the process of purchasing votes in exchange for the spirits. In the center of the line some men are being held up as others still sober are taking them to the voting stations and "helping" them to vote. No, there was no secret ballot in those days.

The only black man in the picture was pouring whiskey. Of course he was not allowed to vote. There are no women at all in this scene. They were also prohibited from voting. There are boys in the picture. They are busy playing marbles but they are present just the same. By the time they are able to vote, the Election Day activities will be very familiar to them.

One thing which does not show in the painting is that each voter had to call out his vote in a loud voice. This was so that no one could change the results. In the center and right side of the painting men can be seen tallying the votes as they are announced. These men were there on behalf of individual candidates just to keep everyone honest. They are the predecessors of today's pole watchers.

The painting on the front of this book is now the property of the St. Louis Art Museum and it is one of the many wonderful paintings which they allow to be viewed for free.

Looking at Mr. Bingham's paintings is one of the best ways to learn about real life in early Missouri. The best places to find original Binghams are the St. Louis Art Museum, the museum at Arrow Rock, Missouri and the State Historical Society of Missouri in Columbia, Missouri. All these places are free and very inspiring.

Want more? One of the best books you'll ever own is a George Caleb Bingham published by Abrams Inc., New York, 1990.

Nineteen: The National Road

Oh, that Thomas Jefferson was a far-sighted man! He envisioned many great things for a great expansive country. One of his visions was for a great National Road to connect the East with the West. In those days the western edge of the U.S. was the Mississippi River so his road was intended to stretch from Washington, D.C. to the river at St. Louis. Then the opportunity came to purchase the Louisiana Territory and double the size of our country, the National Road took on a much larger importance.

It seemed like such a good idea for so many reasons and it wasn't hard to rally support for the idea and soon construction was underway. This was a pretty low-tech process which mostly involved cutting trees, pulling stumps, and some leveling. But it surely was a good idea and it was tackled with enthusiasm. In March, 1806 Congress authorized the building of the road and then, a few months later, Lewis and Clark returned. Their journals were printed and America wanted even more to connect with that vast territory.

Several good toll roads already connected Washington and Baltimore with the western Maryland community of Columbia on the Potomac River. Construction began there at Cumberland in 1811. By 1818 the road stretched to Wheeling, West Virginia. Thanks to Lewis and Clark, Missouri's population was booming and by 1821 Missouri was a state. In 1825 Congress voted to extend the road to St. Louis and Jefferson City.

Time was an enemy of the road, however. Jefferson was gone from office and most of Congress had been replaced because long terms were unknown in those days. New officials had their own new priorities. There was also a new factor in the equation. Railroads were proving to be a safe, inexpensive and comfortable way to move freight and passengers. In 1840 the congress voted against completing the National Road. The great project to link our nation together and connect east and west was stopped at Vandalia, Illinois. That's right – just 70 miles short of its original goal! What would Jefferson have thought?

Then in 1912, the nation had grown so large that the National Road was selected to become a part of a road to be built from New York to San Francisco. The new automobiles were also increasing in use and requiring better quality roads for faster travel. Construction was underway again.

Today you can drive the National Road from Vandalia to Cumberland, Maryland but you probably won't recognize it unless you're watching for historic signs here and there. Most of the signs you see will remind you of the road's new name – U.S. Highway 40. Roughly paralleling that route or even smack on top of it is Interstate Highway 70. Oh, that Thomas Jefferson was a far-sighted man!

Twenty: Annie Malone

People who live near St. Louis hear about the Annie Malone Parade on the first day of May each year. On the TV news they may see the large crowds and all of the happy participants but most aren't even aware of just who Annie Malone was.

In 1869 Annie was born into poverty in Metropolis, Illinois as the 11th of 12 children in her family. This was just four years after the end of the Civil War and, even though she was in Illinois, her parents had been slaves prior to their move to that state. Then while still a child, her parents both died. She went to live with an older sister in Peoria and grew up there.

She had a rough start but, like other great entrepreneurs, she looked at life around her, identified a need, and then systematically addressed that need. The style of the time was for African-Americans to wear their hair straight. They achieved this by coating their hair with goose fat or heavy oils. This worked but it also damaged both the hair and the scalp.

While Annie was still in high school she began experimenting and eventually created a treatment involving applications and a hot comb which would straighten the hair with no un-wanted side effects. And by 1900 her business was growing rapidly. She adopted the brand name "Poro" which is a West African word meaning "physical and spiritual growth."

In 1917 Annie was ready to really unleash her business capabilities. She had already sent an army of salespeople into areas all over America and the Caribbean to sell Poro products door-to-door and at all sorts of gatherings of black women. Then she built a beautiful building in the Ville neighborhood of St. Louis and it housed her new Poro College. It was the first school for black cosmetology in America. Eventually Poro College turned out tens of thousands of trained salespeople who worked all over the world. These women were trained not only in cosmetology but in life skills from how to dress, walk and talk for success but also how to invest wisely.

Annie may have been America's first black multi-millionaire but she also helped thousands of others to become homeowners and savvy investors, secure in their future. Then Annie began to give large sums of money to Howard University and other colleges and endowed scholarships at even more colleges.

Most of all Annie is today remembered for the children's home and orphanage which she started in the 1920s. It would later be named in her honor. A list of alumni from Annie Malone's Children's Home is most impressive indeed. Many of the outstanding citizens who now serve on the board of directors were themselves residents of the home when they were young and in dire need.

So the next time you hear that the Annie Malone parade is happening, remember why this businesswoman, educator, and philanthropist is such an important part of Missouri's heritage.

Twenty-One: Extreme Weather

Weather is always fascinating to people. Extreme weather is even more so. Being right in the middle of a large continent, Missouri is able to enjoy four very distinct seasons but is also subject to all of the extremes of the weather.

The most extreme year would have to have been 1816. Even though good records are not available, that was the famous "Year With No Summer." Because of the eruption of the Mt. Tambora volcano, the earth's atmosphere was filled with ash and gasses. The sun was blocked, the temperatures dropped and the U.S. had snow and freezing temperatures even in June, July, and August. 1881, 1918, and 1936 were three years in which the entire Missouri River from source to mouth were frozen. Ferries couldn't operate so people drove wagons across and in some places, there would be a woodstove kept burning in the middle to help people make the crossing.

Warsaw, Missouri may be the most extreme place of all. They hold the record for the coldest day ever in the state. February 13 of 1905 saw temperatures there plummet to 40° (F) below zero. In that same place they reached the record high of 118° (F) but that was many years later. July 14, 1954 to be exact. Warsaw also has to share that record with Union, Missouri where they reached the same temperature on the same day. Many of us still remember the summer of '54 and what an unbearable time it was before air-conditioning and the like.

Tornadoes have always been a part of Missouri weather lore. On March 18, 1925 what was called "The Tri-State Tornado" ripped through Missouri, Illinois, and Indiana killing 695 people and injuring more than 2000 before finally lifting off the ground. The worst tornado in just Missouri was two years later on May, 9, 1927 when a twister hit Poplar Bluff and killed 93. In that year of 1927 there were a total of 176 Missourians killed by tornadoes. The famous "Night of the Twisters" immortalized in the book and the movie was in 1967 when 45 tornadoes were spawned – 13 of them in Missouri.

Some would have us think that this is a period of global warming and that our heat is setting records all the time. Truth be told, nothing now compares with that summer of 1954 and that doesn't even compare with the entire decade of the 1930s. July of 1930 was the hottest month in Missouri's history.

Now the record for rainfall has many aspects. Little Holt, Missouri claims not only a state record but a world record for rainfall. There, on June 22, 1947 it rained 12 inches in just 42 minutes. That was a real toad strangler! Union, Missouri however, has a claim to more rain in one event. On May 7, 2000 over 14 inches of rain fell in 6 ½ hours in Union.

Snowfall is very hard to rate. One has to consider how much time is involved in a snowstorm, how much snow is already on the ground, whether to factor in other kinds of frozen precipitation during the same event, and so on. I have noticed that snow behaves differently in North Missouri than it does in the southern part of the state. Prairie winds blow the snow and make it do different things in the north. Sloping ground in the south cause it to drift and collect differently in low places than on the hills or knobs. When I think about snow I just have to remember that one on January 31, 1984 when eastern Missouri was smothered with 24-27 inches of snow and it stayed cold enough for us to keep that particular snow on the ground for more than 60 days. That's all the snow I want to think about.

Twenty-Two: Kaskaskia

Kaskaskia, Illinois (or is it Kaskaskia, Missouri?) is one of the most fascinating places in the Midwest. Take a look at the map and you will see that Kaskaskia is on the Missouri side of the Mississippi River. How did that happen?

First let me tell you that Kaskaskia is an important part of Missouri's history. It was the original community from which the French miners came to work in Missouri each day. And, yes, it was on the Illinois side of the river at that time. It's hard to imagine that they would fill their rowboats with iron and other heavy ores and then row across that Mississippi current every day. Of course they eventually decided to settle on the west bank of the river and Ste. Genevieve became Missouri's first permanent settlement.

Kaskaskia is also famous as a frontier outpost. When the Revolutionary War began, George Rogers Clark decided to take it away from the British. Leaving it in their hands would give control of the Mississippi, Missouri, and Ohio River trade routes to the British and strangle any support from the western territories. On July 4th, 1778 Clark entered Fort Gage at Kaskaskia and, due to surprise, took possession without firing a shot. He strolled into a party being given by the English Governor and told the partygoers to continue with their dance, but they were now dancing under Virginia's flag, not England's.

A very old bell which had been a gift of the King of France was rung that day and has come to be known as the Liberty Bell of the West. It can still be seen in the center of town.

Now back to that Missouri/Illinois question. Kaskaskia is definitely on the western bank of the Mississippi but when you drive through there you can't help but notice all of the Illinois license plates on the cars. This is the only part of Illinois which is located on the Missouri side of the River.

In 1811 and 1812 there was a series of earthquakes centered around New Madrid Missouri. These were the most powerful quakes ever recorded in the contiguous states. The first three were 8.0 on the Richter Scale which makes them each 10 times more powerful than the great quake which destroyed San Francisco. During the next two years, thousands of aftershocks shook the ground and there were two new quakes each stronger than any before.

During this time the ground shook so violently that steeples swayed and church bells rang in east coast cities. Large areas sank and filled with water from the Mississippi and created such features as Reelfoot Lake. Other areas rose and lakes disappeared as residents watched. Three great earthen walls rose to completely block the flow of water and the Mississippi began to flow backwards. When it righted itself, the river took a shortcut and separated Kaskaskia from the rest of Illinois. This unique place is fascinating to geologists as well as historians.

Twenty-Three: The "Baddest" Girl of All

You've no doubt heard of the feuding families of Hatfields and McCoys in West Virginia. Well, Myra's mother's family had been the Hatfields. It was 1848 when Myra was born into that rambunctious family now relocated to Carthage, Missouri. Her father, John Shirley was a wealthy inn keeper there in Southwest Missouri. Prior to the Civil War, Missouri and nearby Kansas were involved in a terrible border war and Myra's brother, Bud Shirley left home to join Quantrill's Raiders. In 1864 Bud was killed by Union troops in Sarcoxie, Missouri. Shortly after that, Carthage was burned to the ground.

Before and during the war the teenager, Myra, reported union troop movements to her Confederate friends including Cole Younger (her childhood friend) and Frank and Jesse James. After the war some folks didn't quit fighting. They continued to strike out especially at banks, the Union army, and the railroads. These were three of the major players who had made some people's lives miserable before the war. These Jameses, and Youngers sometimes hid at the Shirley farm so Myra knew them well – especially Cole Younger whom she seems to have loved.

In 1866 Myra married Jim Reed, a former guerilla fighter and they made a home in the Indian Territory which we now call Oklahoma. Jim was not good at farming and soon he fell in with the Starr Clan, a notorious

Cherokee family. Then he got back together with their old outlaw friends from Missouri. Soon Jim committed a murder and then robbed a wealthy Creek Indian of $30,000 in gold coin. Myra was said to have been involved but she claimed to know nothing about it. She took her two children and fled to Texas where she had $30,000 to live a flamboyant life style.

While in Texas she began wearing buckskins and moccasins, or tight black jackets, black velvet skirts, high-topped boots, a man's Stetson hat with an ostrich plume, and twin holstered pistols. She spent her time in saloons drinking and gambling and would sometimes ride through town shooting both pistols. In 1874 Jim rejoined Myra and began robbing stagecoaches. That year he was caught and shot while trying to escape.

Myra left the children with relatives and went back to the Indian Territory where she joined the Starr Clan. At this time Myra also began using her middle name, Belle. Belle's activities in the Indian Territory turned to rustling cattle, stealing horses, and bootlegging whiskey. She was also famous in her role as a hostess to anyone who was running from the law. Her new home was near the borders of Missouri, Kansas, Oklahoma, and Arkansas so she offered the outlaws a valuable service.

In 1880 Belle married Samuel Starr of the Starr Clan and, at that time, she took the name you probably recognize, Belle Starr. Belle was the object of a personal vendetta by Isaac Parker, "the Hanging Judge" but he just couldn't get any major charges to stick.

No one is certain just who it was but someone shot Belle in the back in 1889. Her daughter arranged for a marble headstone on which she had inscribed:

> "Shed not for her the bitter tear,
> Nor give the heart to vain regret;
> 'Tis but the casket that lies here,
> The gem that filled it sparkles yet."

Twenty-Four: Log Homes

Now that people are appreciating the appeal of log homes, the aged oak logs from many old barns and buildings are finding a second life as they are re-used in new homes. The next time you have an opportunity to look at one of these old original homes, take a few minutes and see what stories it can tell. They are as full of personality as were their builders a hundred or more years ago.

The first log homes in Missouri were built by the French settlers in little communities like the one on River Des Peres established in 1700, The Meramec River and Mine LaMotte, and Fort Orleans. Then in 1735, Ste. Genevieve was founded and the population in southeastern Missouri began to grow. All of these early homes had common characteristics.

The most noticeable might be that their walls were made of logs placed upright into trenches and then fastened together. Of course they had to be chinked with clay, twigs, straw, and other materials between the logs but the upright logs were the direct opposite of the horizontal logs which we usually think of in American log buildings.

The French were also good a coping with the heat and humidity. They added large and comfortable porches which they called galleries all the way around their homes. With these there was always a shady spot or a sunny spot to be found depending on your wishes and upon the season. The roofs were thatched at first but later, they would be covered with cedar shingles. Either way the roofs would be steeply sloping to increase the runoff of rainwater and lessen the likelihood of leaks. Being close to river transportation meant that manufactured goods like fine furniture and chandeliers were available for the French log homes.

What is usually called the American Log Cabin was quite different from those of the French. Off course the logs were stacked end-on-end horizontally then holes were drilled down through the ends and wooden pegs were driven deep to anchor the logs together.

Sometimes the homes were constructed as two separate cabins connected with a single porch and roof. The family dogs would sometimes trot under the porch in the summer heat or sleep on the porch on other days so these were called "dog trot" cabins. In a dog trot home you could cook in the "kitchen" building and not heat up the sleeping building. You could also sleep on the porch between the buildings on those really hot summer evenings. Eventually the family could expand their living area by just enclosing the porch space between the two buildings.

A good example of this dog trot style is Grant's Cabin at Grant's Farm near St. Louis. This is a big two-story cabin and the center has been enclosed but it is very easy to see that it was originally constructed as a dog trot home.

In places where the French settlers met up with the American settlers it shows up in the buildings they constructed. The Kelchen family of Franklin County Missouri was surprised as they began to take the modern siding off an outbuilding on their property. They found that, under the siding, was a well-preserved log cabin in two distinct sections. The older section was made with vertical logs and the newer section had its logs stacked horizontally. It's distinct personality resulted from the marriage of the two early cultures between the Missouri and Mississippi Rivers.

Twenty-Five: Mules

Mules have a reputation for being stubborn. They've earned that reputation. They are known for being less than beautiful and for pulling heavy loads. Both of these things are true. The mule is the symbol of Missouri. What else do you know about them? Probably very little. Well, mules are associated with Missouri because at the time when they were most in demand the great majority of all mules came from this state.

Before we go any further, lets talk about what a mule is. It's not really an animal that exists in nature. It is produced when a donkey inseminates a horse. Or you might say a mule's father is a donkey and his mother is a horse. Adult mules almost can't make little ones. My dad used to say that this was nature's way of telling us not to fool around with this kind of stuff.

By crossing these two animals we get a fairly large animal which is patient sure-footed, thick-skinned and is resistant to parasites and weather extremes. Pack mules have been known to carry extremely heavy loads but yoked in a team they do just as well when pulling heavy loads. They tolerate heat, need very little water, and can exist on a lesser quality diet than horses or oxen. In fact, mules have been known to eat such things as tree bark and straw which could never be food for a horse. A good example of their toughness is the 20-mule teams used to haul borax in Death Valley. Some mules bred for Missouri were for the mines. These mining mules weighed about 600 pounds. The big draft mules for pulling might weigh over 1,600 pounds.

We don't know when mules came to Missouri but we do know when they came to the U.S. The first mules in America were a pair of jacks given by the King of Spain as a gift to George Washington. From Virginia these useful animals have come to be produced all across the U.S. but especially in Missouri.

The army was the biggest user of mules. They used them throughout the west and even as late as World War I, mules were indispensable. The army had units called the "40 and 8." In one boxcar they could move a unit of 40 men and just 8 mules to haul all of their food, ammunition, and supplies for a sustained period of duty. About 4000 mules were sent to the army in just the year 1918.

Mules' hooves are very hard and they are recognized by Missouri farmers to be great for pulling farm equipment in clay-filled soil. If you've been fortunate enough to be around mules at any time you have noticed that they can have beautiful coats and can be brushed to a high shine. They can also perform some remarkable physical feats. Standing right next to a very tall fence, mules can on command, jump right over with grace and ease. At one time it was being suggested that the two bears on Missouri's flag be replaced with two mules!

Mule breeders in Missouri and the U.S. now do this as a hobby. In other parts of the world though, they are still in great demand. China and Latin America are the main homes for mules today. It seems however, that the words Missouri and mule will always be together.

Twenty-Six: Moses and Stephen

Try to imagine Stephen's boyhood. He lived in the little mining town of Potosi, Missouri and his father was a very prosperous businessman. His father's store was well-known for fair prices and fair treatment of the customers. Stephen got to play with local children when they weren't working in the mines but he also got to play with the Indian boys whose families also traded at his father's store.

Then one day his father, Moses, announced a strange plan. He said that he would take some supplies and a few horses and travel into the wilderness for thousands of miles through forests, and plains, and deserts, and go all the way to Mexico City. He planned to just drop in and talk with the Spanish Governor of Mexico. As strange as it seems, he did just that. He met with the Governor and offered to solve a problem for Mexico.

The Mexicans just didn't have enough troops to fend off the Indians and protect settlers in the large territory of Texas. Moses explained that he was from Missouri where families were accustomed to holding their own with Indians and they were miners and pioneers who were tough enough that they wouldn't need a big army to protect them.

This meant a fabulous opportunity for Moses' friends back in Missouri. They could sell everything they owned for a profit and then move on to receive large land grants for ranches and farms in Texas. Many jumped at the chance. Then Moses died.

The Mexican legal system called for the eldest son to honor any contracts or agreements made with the father. Now it became the obligation for Stephen to step into this leadership role. He had been elected as a state representative so he was somewhat accustomed to leadership but this was something unique. Finally the day came and Stephen stepped forward and lead several hundred American families toward the Brazos River.

The Americans arrived, staked their claims, and started a town which they named for Stephen. Hard work paid off and the colony thrived. Then Mexico rebelled and overthrew their Spanish overlords. The new dictator, Generalissimo Santa Anna, felt no need to treat the Americans in Texas the same as other Mexican citizens. They spoke a different language, shared a different heritage, and he was afraid that they would someday want to become Americans again. Santa Anna taxed them heavily and put heavy restrictions on their businesses and lives. Missourians and other Americans were not accustomed to be treated this way. The last time that happened, they revolted. And they did again. Stephen went to the U.S. and especially to Washington, D.C. and arranged for loans and aid for the war.

When Texas became an independent nation, they chose the town named for Stephen to be the capital city. So now you know, this 'Father of Texas' who played in the streets and forests around Potosi, was Stephen F. Austin.

Twenty-Seven: Phoebe Apperson

Phoebe was born in Franklin County, Missouri in 1842. I suppose we would say that she lived in poverty but she worked hard, got an education, and prospered. While in Franklin County she taught in a little school south of St. Clair. This little school was made of logs and had only one room.

At age 19 she married her husband, George. George was also from Franklin County. He was home-schooled and graduated from the Franklin County Mining School in 1838. He was more than 20 years older and had gone west to prospect for gold and other minerals in 1850. He was extremely successful. When, in 1860 he came home to care for his ailing mother he met his family's neighbor, Phoebe.

They married and Phoebe moved with George to San Francisco, traveled extensively in Europe, and then moved to another home in Washington, DC when George became a US Senator. Through all of this she never lost her appreciation of education and what it could do for people.

In 1891 she made an extremely large gift to the University of California which provided for buildings and scholarships. Phoebe founded many kindergartens and later financed a school for the training of kindergarten teachers which was a new endeavor at that time. Then in 1897 she founded a group called the National Congress of Mothers which is known today as the P.T.A.

Also this teacher from a log school in Franklin County became the first woman to serve as Regent of the University of California. She built the National Cathedral School for Girls in Washington, DC.

She financed archeological expeditions in Egypt, Peru, Mexico, Europe, and North America and then started a huge museum of anthropology to house the treasures which were discovered.

Phoebe loved to visit castles in Europe so it was no surprise when she decided to build one in the US. In fact, one of her homes is now a California state park. With that clue, you have probably figured out that we've been talking about Phoebe Apperson Hearst.

This young woman from Franklin County became a model for wealthy people of the Gilded Age to use their wealth to help others and to make the world a better place for all. From her home in the Hearst Castle she worked tirelessly as a philanthropist. In 1918 a pandemic of bird flu swept the planet and killed millions of victims. Phoebe died from that deadly illness.

Did she remember her Missouri roots? She certainly did. Just ask any of the St. Clair High School graduates who have gone to college with Hearst scholarships. To find out more about her, visit the Phoebe Apperson Hearst Museum and tour the little log schoolhouse next door. Both are just south of St. Clair.

Twenty-Eight: The Plant Doctor

If you asked someone in the early 1860s who might grow to be a famous Missourian no one would ever think of George Carver. His father died in an accident just before his birth. Then George was born a slave. While he was still an infant, George and his mother were kidnapped by slave raiders who were trying to get them to freedom. George was returned to the plantation but his mother was never heard from again. Who could have had a worse start in life than an orphaned slave baby?

It got worse. He was so sickly and frail that he couldn't do the work which was required of him. Then, with slavery ended, he was on his own – a sickly child with no one to look after him and not even a slave owner to train him to be useful.

He began doing housework and gardening to earn his keep. In spare time he wandered through the woods and his interest in plants grew. People recognized his knack for helping ailing plants and began to call the boy "the plant doctor." Someone at his home taught him to read and write and he was a fast and willing learner.

Little Diamond, Missouri had no schools for black children so, at age 10 George left to search for a school. Can you imagine a 10-year-old boy with no experiences more than a couple of miles from his home just walking off into the countryside in search of his education and his life? What thoughts must have filled his head!

He traveled to Neosho, Missouri where he found a little school and a way to earn a living while he studied. He was accepted into a college in Kansas but when he got there they realized he was black and turned him away. George kept looking until he arrived in Indianola, Iowa. There he enrolled in Simpson College to study piano and painting. He loved the world of fine arts and excelled in music.

In 1891 an instructor recognized George's abilities in botany and encouraged him to be a little more pragmatic. She emphasized how horticulture would provide a much more secure future than music. Following her advice, he became the first black man to enroll in what is now Iowa State University. When he began taking classes he discovered that there was another George Carver in his classes. The campus post office sometimes mixed up the mail for the two Georges. Our George solved the problem by changing his name. He claims to have been an admirer of our first president so began using the name of George Washington Carver.

His college career was enough to make a movie but the important thing is that he earned two degrees, published articles about his research, and distinguished himself in plant science. His fame caused him to be noticed by Booker T. Washington who invited George to join the faculty at the Tuskegee Institute. Here he made scientific history.

He invented hundreds of new products and uses for crops which would enrich the soil of the south. One of the greatest scientists and inventors of our time began life as a baby slave and at 10-years-old began wandering the heartland in search of knowledge. Even as a child, he was a person filled with great dreams.

Twenty-Nine: The Great Rivers

You've heard the expression, "Missouri, where the rivers run." We are blessed with abundant rain and it makes our farms productive. It makes our lives free of the water worries that others have. If you've ever traveled in the west, you know how good it feels to get back to Missouri's lush greenness. Of course we also have this abundance of lakes and rivers.

How much do you know about our rivers? For instance, Missouri is the meeting place of the two biggest rivers on the North American continent. Can you name them? That was too easy. How about this one? Missouri's borders with Iowa and Arkansas are just lines that politicians drew on a map. Four other parts of our borders are natural borders formed by rivers. Can you name the four rivers which form Missouri's borders? I'll give you a minute.

Try this one. Which river is the primary source for the water which fills the Lake of the Ozarks? Here's a hint. This same river also forms Truman Lake.

Here's a tricky one. Be careful. Where is the mouth of the Missouri River?

OK, I'll throw in an easy one. What is it that carved out the Meramec Caverns? Yes, it's a river but which one?

When Jefferson City was chosen as the state's capital city, it was because of a directive that the capital be near the junction of which two great rivers? In those days the rivers were the state's best roads. Which two great river roads come together near Jefferson City?

The Hudson River school was a group of artists who said that American landscapes were just as inspiring as European landscapes. Then one artist declared that the Missouri River was just as interesting as any. Who was this greatest of all Missouri artists who painted so many scenes of river life and the boatmen? Who is probably today's greatest artist actively painting Missouri river scenes?

OK let's see how you did. The great artist who painted our state's river history was George Caleb Bingham. His best counterpart today is probably Gary Lucy of Washington, Missouri.

How about the two rivers near Jefferson City? That would be the Missouri of course and also the Osage River. Meramec Caverns was and still is being formed by . . . . the Meramec River. The tricky one about the mouth of the Missouri River – it's just north of St. Louis. I did say the "mouth" of the river, not the source.

Which river forms the Lake of the Ozarks? It's the Osage again. It's an important one isn't it?

Finally, did you know the four rivers which form our state's boundaries? The first two are easy. The Mississippi forms our eastern border. The Missouri forms much of our western border. Then, down in the southeast, the entire western side of the Bootheel is formed by the St. Francois River. In the northeast corner, just a few miles of our border is formed by the Des Moines River. Try to remember those four – they make good borders and good trivia questions.

Thirty: Our First Superstar

William was a Virginian and proud of it. He was the younger brother of a true hero of The Revolution. William also chose a military career and was a respected young officer. Life was good. It got even better when he met the lovely red-headed Virginia socialite, Julia Hancock. He was on the fast track for the good life.

Then he met another young Virginian who asked him to risk everything including his very life and go on what may have been one of the greatest adventures in the history of the world. I would put Marco Polo's travels in that category as well as the first expedition to walk on the moon. And then – this.

The other young man was a brilliant naturalist, probably manic-depressive, and definitely in over his head. He had been given the rank of Captain for this adventure but he needed the help of a true army officer. William was the perfect choice.

These two led a group of men far away from the last outpost of civilization and into a totally unknown part of the world. As they say on Star Trek, their mission was to explore this New World, encounter strange civilizations, and go where no known man had gone before. Of course I'm talking about the Corps of Discovery and the leaders, Meriwether Lewis and our William – William Clark.

Clark did a masterful job and long after they were given up for dead, they returned to St. Louis and a hero's welcome. Most know about what William did on that Voyage of Discovery but not so many know what he did afterwards.

When he got back to St. Louis he immediately got his papers in order and submitted them to President Jefferson and then his next item was to marry his Julia. That done, he brought her back to St. Louis where they would live for the rest of their lives. Clark was appointed the Agent for Indian Affairs, then Brigadier General of the Missouri Militia. For seven years he was the Governor of Missouri. After his time as Governor, he went back to work in Indian affairs and was well-known for his fair treatment of the Indians. He may be a major reason why Missouri had almost none of the Indian strife which was common in other parts of the east and west.

William Clark became one of the primary reasons for the growth and prosperity of Missouri and was the state's first super star hero. His maps and journals were so clear and accurate that people from all over the world began making plans to see this new place and a flood of immigration began. There may have been no one person more responsible for Missouri's early growth than William Clark.

William died in 1838 in St. Louis and is buried under a beautiful monument in Bellefontaine Cemetery along with most of St. Louis' early heroes.

Thirty One: A Great Engineer

James was born in Indiana in 1820 and by the age of 10 was showing a real interest in mechanical things. He was already building models of sawmills, fire engines, and steamboats by the time he moved to St. Louis at age 13. In 1833 St. Louis was an American town, rather smallish, with a strong French flavor. Lewis and Clark had done their expedition and the word was out about the gateway city but the Irish, Germans and others had not yet arrived.

As a young man James recognized that a fortune was sitting at the bottom of the Mississippi River because the wooden-hulled boats were sinking routinely, cargo and all. He began to experiment with a device which worked like an upside down glass placed in water. It trapped air inside. He called this a diving bell and taught salvage divers how to use it for breathing while they retrieved the treasure that others had given up for lost. He was soon a very wealthy man. Then he invented a method for pumping the sand and water out of the sunken vessels and raising not only the treasure but the boat itself. With some repairs, he soon had his own fleet of abandoned but perfectly good riverboats.

At age 24 the young James went to visit his cousin who had married a prominent widower. There he met the widower's daughter, Martha Dillon. After courting for a time he asked her to marry him. Martha was willing but her father was not. He forbade her from marrying James because he was not from a sufficiently important family. This was a little funny for a couple of reasons. Martha's father had himself married into that family – remember, his wife was James' first cousin. The other funny thing is that James was named for his uncle James Buchanan, the President of the United States!

A year later she went against her father's wishes and married James. That was also the year, 1855, that James sold his riverboat and salvage interests and started the first glassworks west of the Mississippi. Then in 1861 he was called to Washington and asked to help in the Civil War. He contracted to build eight ironclad steamers equipped as gunboats. He finished this job in just 100 days and a full month earlier than the battle between the Monitor and the Merrimac. Then he produced many more gunboats to help in the siege of Vicksburg and Admiral Farragut's capture of Mobile.

After the war he became obsessed with doing the impossible. He wanted to build a bridge across the Mississippi at St. Louis. Some told him it was impossible. The river was too wide and the current too powerful. Others told him that, for his own safety, he had better not offend the ferryboat operators. Most of all he was told to drop the silly notion of building the bridge of steel.

The crowning achievement of this man's life is the triple-arched bridge which still stands today carrying cars, pedestrians, and metrolink commuter trains across the Father of Waters. Now you know, the wonderful old Eads Bridge is named for one of our greatest engineers, James Buchanan Eads.

Thirty Two: The King of Ragtime

Just after the end of the Civil War Scott was born into a struggling family in Texarkana. His family lived at times on both sides of the state line. His mother worked as a cleaning lady for a German family and, while Mom worked, Scott began to teach himself to play tunes on the German family's piano. Julius Weiss recognized his talent and began instructing him. This was the beginning of a musical legend.

For a reason unknown Scott's family moved to Sedalia, Missouri and Scott was introduced to a new kind of jazz played mostly on the piano and it was usually fast-moving and cheerful. Its primary home was Sedalia and it was called Ragtime.

Scott was very good at playing this new kind of music and was very much in demand around Sedalia. In addition to just playing the piano, he was attending high school and then the George R. Smith College in

Sedalia where he studied music theory. Soon he was writing his own arrangements and composing his own tunes.

These Ragtime compositions found their way to various printers and were soon selling all over the United States. The young composer came to be hailed as "The King of Ragtime." He spent a good part of his life in St. Louis with other jazz and ragtime musicians and this is where his publisher lived. The most special time in St. Louis was in 1904 when he played regularly at the World's Fair.

His popularity brought him job offers to play in many places like St. Louis, Chicago, and New York. The big problem was that, even though he made money and got fame from his composing, he still had to play the piano to pay the bills. As the years went by the time he spent in sleazy places took a toll on him. He contracted syphilis during his youth and that disease would ultimately bring debilitation and his early death.

Within a few years the music we know now as jazz had replaced ragtime in popularity and Scott spent his last years in obscurity. Then in the 1970s the movie, The Sting, used his music throughout and ragtime was reborn and an interest in Scott was renewed more than half a century after his death. By now you know that I've been describing the life of Scott Joplin who truly was The King of Ragtime.

He is remembered now for his genius. His songs like *The Maple Leaf Rag* (named for the Maple Leaf Social Club in Sedalia) and *The Entertainer* are recognized by everyone. Joplin received the Pulitzer Prize for his opera, Treemonisha which was based on his own life. Now Scott Joplin's home in St. Louis is a state historical site operated as a part of the State Parks system. Each year the folks at Sedalia hold a Ragtime Festival where everyone knows Scott Joplin's achievements.

Ragtime music has been reborn and so has the memory of Scott Joplin. He was the best of the best at this new form of music that, like its master, grew up in the Heartland.

Thirty Three: The Runaway Saddle Maker

When the Boone family came to Missouri along with the Bryans, Callaways, and others it began a migration from Kentucky and Tennessee into Missouri. In this migration was the family of little 3-year-old Christopher. Christopher's family first moved to one of the forts between St. Charles and Boon's Lick. Soon they moved to another fort and then to a third. Finally they moved to a little town just getting started on the north bank of the Missouri River. This was Franklin, Missouri, the eastern end of the Santa Fe Trail.

Trying to do the right thing, Christopher's father arranged for him to apprentice to a craftsman in the area. At age 14, it was time for Christopher to learn a trade and being a saddle maker was an excellent opportunity to work into a career. In fact making leather goods should provide a safe and comfortable living for the rest of his life.

All Christopher could think of was how boring it seemed to be tied down to a business for his whole life. He grew up with the Boones. He wanted adventure. He wanted fame and fortune. He wanted out. So, in 1815, he ran away.

Now, I'm guessing that he was not a very good apprentice because the saddle maker did offer a reward for the return of the boy but the reward he offered was only one cent. Of course nobody wanted to chase him down and drag him back for just a penny.

Christopher worked his way into the west by signing on to a wagon train going west on the Santa Fe Trail. He loved the adventure and he found that he had a skill with languages. In addition to English he soon could speak Spanish, Navaho, Apache, Cheyenne, Arapahoe, Paiute, Shoshone, and Ute.

His life was full of adventure and his travels took him over all areas of the far west. He served as a guide for John C. Fremont and for Stephen W. Kearny. He also served as a guide for wagon trains taking manufactured goods and settlers into the west and bringing gold, silver, and furs back to Missouri.

After serving as a guide for the US Army, he was given command of 500 men during the Civil War and achieved the rank of General. He later served as Superintendent of Indian Affairs in the Colorado Territory. His first wife was, in fact, an Arapahoe woman and, after her death, he married a Cheyenne woman. .

This man who was such a failure at making leather goods had one of the greatest lives of adventure in our country's history. If you look through the west you will find a state capital city, a national forest, mountain passes, trails, counties, schools, valleys, highways, parks, a mountain and many cities named for this man from Franklin, Missouri. His life has been told in dime novels, poems, books, comic books, and movies. Most people don't call him Christopher but know him by his nickname, Kit - Kit Carson.

Thirty Four: The Evolution of Roads

The very first roads in Missouri are still with us today. The Indians used the great rivers of the state to get from place to place and to link their communities together. The explorers used these rivers to see as much of the land as possible in their limited time. Then the pioneers and settlers began building homes and starting farms and towns along the Mississippi and the Missouri and later the tributaries to these two. Glancing at the map shows how all of the earliest commerce and development happened on the banks of the two biggest rivers in North America.

The Indians also made trails to connect communities and hunting grounds which were not on flowing water. These came to be used by the white men and then improved to become roads and some are even highways today.

The first actual roads in Missouri were built to connect the areas around Ste. Genevieve and Ironton. These roads were needed to carry minerals from the mines to the rivers for shipment south. They were often built at "Road Bees" where neighbors would gather and work together for a common good. As with all early roads they were rutted and hard to use. After a rain the wagon ruts would be so deep that travel would be almost impossible.

The first step in creating a road would be to cut down the trees which stood in the way. They would have to be cut low enough that the wagon axles could straddle the stumps. As the ruts grew deeper, the stumps seemed to protrude higher and higher. The time would come when wagons would begin to scrape to a stop on top of the stumps. The wagon master would try to back off and then go forward and sometimes nothing seemed to work and he didn't know what to do. He might then be heard to say, "Now I'm stumped."

One solution was to fell trees across the road and place them side-by-side. This was called a corduroy road. It solved some problems but it's hard to imagine how jarring and uncomfortable it must have been to ride on this surface. Then some genius thought to cut the logs in half and lay them with the smoother side up. This meant that you only needed to cut half as many trees and the surface of the road was much smoother! Reminders of these Plank Roads can still be found around Ste. Genevieve and Farmington.

It soon became profitable to build a short railroad from Ste. Genevieve to the mines of the Mineral Area. This road had rails and a powerful engine could pull increasingly heavy loads of ore, logs, granite, and passengers.

By the time of the St. Louis World's fair in 1904 most of America's roads were still just made of dirt. The coming of the automobile brought a demand for better roads and paved highways. A good example of the development of our roads is the Osage Trail from St. Louis to Springfield.

The Osage had a foot trail stretching from the mounds of St. Louis to the good hunting prairie and springs around where Lebanon, Marshfield, and Springfield are today. This came to be used by pioneers on horseback and then trees were cleared by the army to make a road and it was called The Military Road. When a telegraph wire was first stretched, some folks began to call it The Wire Road. As demand grew Congress mandated the building of Route 66 and, of course, that became today's Interstate 44. All along the old Osage Trail.

The Center State
Missouri is at the center of the 48 contiguous states.

Thirty Five: Nicknames

Missouri has no official nickname. We are known as "The Show Me State." This comes from our stubbornness and our refusal to accept things just because someone tells them to us. There are differing stories about how this nickname came about and, contrary to popular belief, it is not the official nickname of the state. Of course it does appear on our license plates.

Many people would like to have some of our other nicknames on the license plates. Those interested in tourism would like for us to be known as "The Cave State." Missouri does have cave state license plates available to anyone who requests them. The Cave State has over 7,000 caves and many of them are commercially developed.

Many folks are concerned about Missouri's identity. Are we a western state, a southern state, a northern state, a plains state, or what? These folks favor another nickname for Missouri – "The Center State." This is a pretty good one. Glancing at a map will show that between the Gulf of Mexico and Missouri there are two states. There are also two states between us and Canada. Looking east we see that there are five states between us and the Atlantic Ocean. There are also five states between us and the Pacific Ocean. We are truly in the center of the contiguous states! One additional point for The Center State argument is that the population center of the United States in Steeleville, Missouri.

Here's something else fun to do with Missouri on a map. If you can locate a small map of the United States (or use the one on the previous page), color Missouri red. Then color Arkansas blue. Next carefully color Louisiana brown. Be sure to color all of Louisiana including that part that sticks out eastward into the Gulf of Mexico. Then color Minnesota blue. Finally, carefully use any colors you like and make a little profile head out of the state of Iowa. Do you see the nose on the east. Give him some hair and a mouth and an eye. Now you've got a pudgy little man with a big floppy hat right in the center of the states.

Many of Missouri's nicknames have come from the mining industry in the southern half of the state. It has been called "The Iron Mountain State," "The Bullion State," and "The Lead State." It once promoted itself as "The Pennsylvania of the West."

Belle Starr and her friends like Cole Younger and Frank and Jesse James earned Missouri the nickname of "The Outlaw State." During the border war, the militia from Iowa corrupted the name of Pike County and called Missouri "The Puke State." I haven't seen a call to put that one on license plates.

The nickname which has the most meaning for me becomes obvious as you look at maps of the western U.S. and see all of the names of Missouri places and people duplicated over and over again. I like Missouri's nickname, "Mother of the West."

Thirty Six: Riverboats

In the early days Indians used Missouri's great rivers as their highways. When Europeans arrived they did the same. As time went by the boats changed in appearance but, even today, some of the busiest and most important roads in the state are liquid.

The name Missouri is an Illini Indian word meaning "land of big canoes." The Osage and Missouri tribes did in fact use very big canoes. Not the little birch bark things which might come to mind. These big canoes were made by burning away the bottom of some large trees and hacking away at them until they fell in or near the water. Then fires would be set to slowly burn away the inside of the tree. The ends of the log would be sharpened and a gigantic canoe was ready.

White men like the trappers used the big canoes also to haul their furs back to market. Then the settlers came and they began to build flatboats. They were so flat on the bottom that they could go in the shallowest of water. One man could steer them with an oar but it would take several men to pull them from the shore or to push them using long poles stuck into the river bottom. These flatboats could only go downstream, never upstream, so they were disassembled and sold for lumber when they got to their destination.

Keelboats could travel upstream. They were built with a ribbed framework attached to a center keel which allowed them to knife though the water. They still had to be pulled upstream. Occasionally if conditions were just right, a small sail could help. Only the strongest and toughest of men could work on these boats.

Then Dewitt Clinton thought of putting a steam engine on a keelboat and the steamboat was born. This changed everything! Now a trip upstream from New Orleans could be a leisurely even luxurious affair. Men began thinking it possible to bring their families up to the middle of the continent. St. Louis became a destination and a jumping off place for settlers, merchants, and families of all types.

There were two types of steamboats. One had its paddlewheel in the back and it worked very well. It was called a "sternwheeler." The other kind was a "side-wheeler" because its paddlewheels were on each side. This type was just as good and it was much more maneuverable. It made it much easier to dock in places like St. Louis where "parking" places were cramped and the sideways current constantly worked against the riverboat pilot.

As time went by, competition increased and riverboats began competing for speed, luxury, and entertainment. A trip on a steamboat could be a wonderful thing! Today there are still several passenger-carrying riverboats on Missouri's waters and many towboats hauling coal and grain to demanding markets from our American heartland.

The Little Country Church
St. John's Mantels

Thirty Seven: The Little Country Church

Somehow I got to be the historian at a little country church. I didn't ask for the job and I wasn't elected or chosen or asked. It's just that the church was about to observe its 150th birthday and someone needed to collect its history. I want to share a little of what I found.

There is a little stream which runs in the valley on the church's property. That stream was named by Lewis and Clark in 1804. It was named for a French trapper who was working at the mouth of the stream when the explorers came through.

In 1836 there was no church in the area but the settlers were meeting in a big log barn owned by one of the families involved. In nice weather they would meet under a tree. Later they found a circuit rider. This was a traveling preacher who rode around the frontier, meeting and living with groups of Christians.

In 1841, there was a national depression and a farmer next door to the barn couldn't pay his taxes and he abandoned his farm to move west and start over. The church members organized and purchased the land for taxes. A church building was constructed of logs and the pioneers' church was now real and solid.

In 1848, gold was discovered in California and people poured into St. Louis waiting in that gateway city for the Spring and a chance to rush west. Too many people in such a small place resulted in a cholera epidemic. As the '49ers left St. Louis many of them made it no farther than the next county before they died of cholera. Those people are buried in mass graves consisting of two long un-marked trenches at the little church. The church's two cemeteries also hold the graves of 34 veterans of the War Between the States.

In the early days the church was part of a group of churches which formed in the Missouri Valley. This confederation demanded that member churches have at least 40 acres of land. That would be enough that, with careful harvesting and re-planting, there should be plenty of oak to heat a church and a parsonage. These prudent and pragmatic pioneers purchased 80 acres just to be sure.

In those early days, the women and younger children would go into church as soon as they arrived and sit on the left side of the sanctuary. The men and older boys waited outside with the horses until the bell rang signaling that it was time for them to come in for service. They sat on the right. We did things this way on our 160th anniversary and the responsive readings and hymns had a totally different sound. It was great!

Why am I telling you all of this? Well there is a lot more, believe me. But also there is a lot of history in many places around the state if people will take the time to find out and especially to write it down. What tales from the heartland might you be able to find out about?

Thirty Eight: The Heatherly War

In the entire history of the Midwest it could be that the most despicable group of people of all were the Heatherlys. This family of desperadoes did everything they could to start a war. It has come to be known as the Heatherly War.

The Heatherlys lived in the area of the upper Grand River in what would now be Carroll, Mercer, and Grundy Counties. The year was 1836 and this part of Missouri was considered to be way out on the frontier. George Heatherly was on the run from authorities in Kentucky. His wife, Jenny, was the sister of colorful brothers called Big and Little Harpe. They were the worst of Kentucky's worst. At their homestead they also had living several fugitives from eastern states.

This Jenny Heatherly was said to be the cruel brains of the outfit but she was just so terrible that it may be her reputation surpassed her deeds. For a time, anything bad that happened in the upper Grand River area was blamed on Jenny, her family, and her followers.

There are several stories about exactly what happened in June of 1836 but it seems fairly certain that a group of Pottawatomie Indians came down from Iowa either hunting or migrating west. The Heatherlys tried to sell them some moonshine whiskey but the Indians refused. Determined to somehow make a profit, the Heatherlys went back to the Indian camp and stole several horses. Shots rang out and one of the gang fell dead. The others retreated leaving the horses for the Pottawatomies.

The Heatherlys then murdered James Dunbar, the one man who had a conscience and might be persuaded to talk and, with that taken care of, they traveled south to report the incident to other settlers. Of course their telling of it had them be the innocent victims of a raiding party which preceded thousands of warriors. The state militia was called from neighboring counties and they proceeded north to wage war.

Fortunately cool heads prevailed and when the thousands of braves could not be found, people began to question the story of the Heatherlys. Soon the little band of Pottawatomie were discovered at their camp. It became clear that the Indians were not the troublemakers but the intended victims.

Warrants were issued for the arrests of the Heatherly family and all of the accomplices in the murder of James Dunbar. There was no jail in that county at the time so the prisoners were distributed to sheriffs throughout the area to await trial. Without any real proof the Heatherlys were acquitted of the crime but remained afraid of future troubles so they decided to testify against their gang member, Alfred Hawkins, and make him a scapegoat. Eventually Hawkins was found guilty and served two years before he died in prison. This ended what came to be known as the Heatherly War. It seems to have been given that title so the militia involved could get paid and get credit for their service.

And what became of the Heatherlys? No one knows. But they were getting pretty good at running from one place to another when their deeds caught up with them.

Thirty Nine: The Heartland's Biggest Party

Some people really know how to throw a party! Of course it helps to have an occasion to celebrate. In this case it was the 100th anniversary of the Lewis and Clark Expedition. Let me tell you about some of the things which made this party special.

One Missouri physician was concerned about his patients who had lost their teeth. How could he help them to get protein into their diets? For them he introduced peanut butter.

One ice cream vendor ran out of bowls so he went to a waffle vendor and ordered waffles which he rolled up and called an ice cream cone.

Sausages had been around forever but this time they were served on special long buns and called hot dogs. Another man took a hot drink and adapted it to Missouri's summer heat and iced tea was born. Cotton Candy (called Fairy Floss at this party) was first sold in quantity. Hot dogs, hamburgers, Dr. Pepper, cotton candy, and iced tea had all been served to small groups of people prior to the party but this was the place where they were introduced to the general public.

Almost every country and culture in the world sent someone to the party. The entire world was invited. World leaders and royalty flooded into St. Louis. Trains carried people from everywhere to attend.

In addition to all of the other entertainment and contests, the Summer Olympics were held as one small part of this giant event. Another entertainment feature included all kinds of rides. One Ferris wheel was so huge that it had 36 cars which each held 60 passengers. When it turned it carried 2,160 people at a time. It's hard to imagine that when it was brought to the party, it had to be carried on 175 railroad flatbed cars. The axle alone weight 70 tons!

Many incredibly beautiful buildings were created from plaster just for the party and then torn down immediately afterwards. For some, the "highlight" was the lights themselves. For many people this was the first time to see electric lights. The old song about the event said, "Don't tell me the lights are shining anywhere but there." Everyone went home after spending summer evenings under the lights and demanded lights for their hometowns also.

By now you have realized that this party celebrating the 100th anniversary of the Lewis and Clark Expedition was also Missouri's way of saying to the world, "Look at us. We've arrived on the world stage." It was called the Louisiana Purchase Exposition but we all know it as the 1904 St. Louis World's Fair.

Forty: Aviation Pioneers and Milestones

Everyone has heard of The Spirit of St. Louis." This was Lucky Lindy's famous plane in which he soloed the Atlantic and put his name into the history books. But do you know why the plane had such a name?

When the US Postal Service decided to consider carrying the mail by air they tried a limited mail route to see if it was practical. That first mail route went between South St. Louis and North St. Louis. Then the expanded air mail service opened routes between all sorts of places such as between St. Louis and Chicago. The Robertson Aircraft Corporation of St. Louis won that contract and hired young Charles Lindbergh to do the flying. He was a pilot in the Missouri National Guard.

When Lindbergh decided to try for the transatlantic prize he asked St. Louisans to help him build a plane for the occasion. His first backer was Major Albert Lambert who operated an airport at his own expense on his property just west of St. Louis. Soon other enthusiastic people from the area chipped in and soon Lindbergh was able to purchase a Wright Whirlwind and modify it for the special task of non-stop flight.

After completing his journey, Lindbergh flew his plane back to St. Louis and landed at Mr. Lambert's airfield. Missourians were so excited about aviation that they adopted a $2,000,000 bond issue to buy and maintain what is now Lambert International Airport.

Before Lindbergh's time much of the world's interest in aviation was focused on balloons and dirigibles. The St. Louis Aero Club sponsored the "Great American Air Meet" which featured dirigible races in 1908 and in 1910 airplanes were to gain the most interest in this international competition. An astonishing record of 60 mph was established at this 1910 event. Remember, these events were only 5 and eight years after the Wright Brothers' first flight at Kitty Hawk.

History was also made at the 1910 event when Theodore Roosevelt decided that he wanted to fly in an airplane. He came to St. Louis for this landmark event in aviation. Flying was becoming respectable and somewhat safe. In 1912, Captain Berry came to St. Louis to make the very first parachute jump from a moving airplane. In 1916 the first Army Air Corps was established in St. Louis. Soon people were realizing that the location and climate which made St. Louis such a good place for aviation also made Kansas City a great location and aviation made the jump to that city in a big way. Over the 100 plus years of aviation history these two Missouri cities have been the bases of operations for several commercial airlines.

In the early 20th century ballooning and aircraft records were being set in St. Louis and in the early 21st century ballooning and aircraft records were still being established from St. Louis with the adventurer, Steve Fossett. Among other things he was the first to fly an airplane around the world non-stop. He worked through Washington University. St. Louis University also has an aviation interest with the Parks-St. Louis Airport.

James McDonnell located his McDonnell-Douglas Aircraft corporation in St. Louis on Lindbergh Boulevard at Lambert Field. Here they made not only great airplanes but they also took America into the Space Age with almost all of the earliest space ships. One last Missouri – Aviation thought. There is only one place in the world where B-1 stealth bombers are based. Your guessed it – Whiteman Air Force Base in Central Missouri.

Forty One: Music in the Heartland

It's a funny thing how people around the world know much about the music in Missouri's history but few Missourians seem to realize its significance. Now if you mention music in Missouri lots of folks think of rock concerts in St. Louis or Kansas City or the elaborate musical stage shows at Branson might come to mind. There's much more!

For instance, where would you find the oldest symphony orchestra in America? Well there's a question about that because a military post band was once formed in New Orleans and it became the New Orleans Symphony but it went out of business for a while. The next oldest group is the St. Louis Symphony Orchestra but it has been continuously active longer than any other musical group in the country.

Then there's jazz. One early form is called Ragtime and its principal composer and performer was Scott Joplin who centered his professional life around Sedalia and St. Louis. Jazz was not widely accepted and respected however until the publication and recording of the St. Louis Blues on the Mississippi riverboats. One of St. Louis' nicknames is "Home of the Blues" and that doesn't mean the hockey team. St. Louis has continued to be a center of jazz right up through modern times with native sons like Miles Davis leading the way. Of course Kansas City was and still is a leading jazz city. Its most famous performer was probably Count Basie.

The Beatles' Paul McCartney said that if Rock and Roll had a different name, that name would probably have to be Chuck Berry Music. In addition to his pioneering Rock & Roll works, Berry still performs regularly in the St. Louis area. This very first inductee into the Rock and Roll Hall of Fame also wrote music for other groups such as the Beatles and the Beach Boys.

One of the most interesting developments in our state's musical heritage came from two sources. First was that group of Scots-Irish settlers who came here from Appalachia and brought fiddles, guitars, and harps from the old country. Here in America they traded the harp for other stringed instruments and introduced the banjo to create our own folk music. There are still many places where this Missouri variety of Bluegrass music is performed at the drop of a hat.

The second part of this story is the music which came up from the southwest in cattle drives and later along Route 66. The cowboys and vaqueros had their own musical style and it used many of the same instruments as the country music which was already here. With time these two musical styles melded together and Country-Western Music was born.

In the early days of television, many aspiring young country-western stars would make their way to Springfield, Missouri for an audition with Red Foley. They were hoping to get a spot on The Ozark Jubilee, a nationally-televised program which gave Porter Waggoner, Dolly Parton, and many others their starts. This toe-tapping tradition is carried on today in Branson and all over the state.

Forty Two: A Family's Good Name

In the southern section of Laclede County is the little community of Russ. In Russ there is what remains of a log church named the Gilead Baptist Church. The logs have all been consumed by nature's decomposers and all that remains are stones. A few stones show where the foundation was and a few other stones mark graves from long ago. One tall grave stone is a monument to the pioneer Albert Hamilton.

On Albert's tombstone it says, "A good name is rather to be chosen than great riches." When I first saw these carved words it didn't mean much to me. It was just a quotation from Proverbs which anyone might like on their headstone. Then I found out more about Albert and I understood why this was a huge part of who he was.

Before coming to Missouri Albert lived in Barren County, Kentucky. He was the son of a very prosperous man who owned many farms. Albert and his brother, John C., grew up there and learned the business of running a large operation in three adjoining counties.

One day a man arrived on horseback. He was up from Alabama and was looking for horses there in the Bluegrass State. Albert's brother John C. took an instant liking to this man and they became fast friends. John

C. showed the stranger around the countryside and introduced him to many breeders.

Then the news came that the wealthy stranger had been murdered and robbed. His friend, John C. had been traveling with him earlier and was aware of the money that the stranger carried. Then they found the hidden blood-stained coveralls – John C.'s coveralls. Now, a farmhand said that he had used John C.'s coveralls while they butchered a pig and was afraid to put them back since they were covered with blood and ruined. Many did not believe the farmhand's testimony.

Betting was underway all over Barron County. Some bet that a rich man would never hang in that area. Others felt it important to show that justice was blind and that no one was above the law. Records show a flurry of activity over a period of three years as the Hamilton family bought and sold land and then personal possessions, sacrificing everything in order to pay ever-increasing legal bills and lobbying for mercy.

Finally after a verdict of "guilty" and several appeals John C. Hamilton was hung. The family was shamed, disgraced, and broke. Albert made plans to leave for Missouri with his daughter and son-in-law. They hadn't been here long when news came from distant Mississippi that another man was being hung when he decided to clear his conscience and confess his other crimes also. He described in detail a murder he had committed in Kentucky in which he ambushed and robbed a rich man then left him by the road. The people in Barron County had hung the wrong man.

People came to Missouri for many reasons. Some for adventure, some for escape, most came for economic opportunity. Albert Hamilton came to Missouri in disgrace hoping to once again have a good name and the respect he deserved. He knew even better than most of us that, "A good name is rather to be chosen than great riches."

Forty Three: Presidents from Missouri

Can you name the presidents who came from Missouri? Oh, you thought there was only one? Well, Harry S Truman was surely a U.S. President. His nickname was indeed, the Man From Missouri. Did you know that most people in Missouri or anywhere else can't spell this man's name correctly? It's that "S" in the middle. Everyone wants to put a period after the "S" but that's wrong. It's not an initial – it's a name. His middle name is "S" so a period after it is not appropriate.

So who else? I'll bet you've been to the Missouri home of another president. On Gravois Road in St. Louis County sits the impressive log home of Ulysses S. Grant. He wasn't a president while he lived here but he <u>did</u> live here and he certainly <u>was</u> a president.

Now it gets tricky. There was actually a third Missourian who could claim to have been President of the United States – at least for a while. It happened that the elected president, Zachary Taylor, refused to be inaugurated on March 4, 1849 as he should have. That date was a Sunday and he insisted on waiting until Monday. That left the United States without a president for one day. The Vice President couldn't take over because, he too was supposed to be inaugurated on the same day as the President. Under the Constitution as it stood at that time, the next person in line of succession was the President Pro-Tempore of the Senate. This man was Missourian, David Rice Atchison.

So, yes, some say that this third Missourian was president for a day and it even says that on his grave monument but he was never sworn in or even conducted any business at all on that day. All in all, it's just a good fact for a trivia question.

Atchison's life however, was not trivial. This man went to college at Transylvania University where five of the men in his small graduating class were to become US Senators and one became the President of the Confederacy. In 1830 he moved to Liberty, Missouri and set up a law practice. Four years later he was elected to the Missouri Legislature to fight for the annexation of the northwestern corner of the state. Prior to his time, the western border of the state was a straight line north and south. He was instrumental in adding the territory out to the Missouri River.

He served as a General and quenched the violence in the Mormon War. He also advocated for statehood for Kansas, Nebraska, and Texas. To help in this, he founded the city of Atchison in Atchison County, Kansas and therefore, the Atchison, Topeka and the Santa Fe Railway. Of course, Atchison County, Missouri is named for him also. I guess that we could say he was pragmatic but the truth is that he felt that the ends justified the means and he did some outrageous things to get his way.

Atchison will always be remembered for getting the Transcontinental Railroad to take a northern route which included Missouri rather than Texas. He will also be remembered for his duty with Sterling Price in the Civil War. This Senator-General-"President" personally shaped the geography and history of four western states.

Section of the Berlin Wall
Westminster College, Fulton

The Columns
University of Missouri, Columbia

Forty Four: Missouri Icons

When I say St. Louis, you probably think of the Gateway Arch. Some places are identified in our minds with particular landmarks or monuments. Many cities in Missouri have famous things which form an important part of the identity of those places.

When people try to get a mental picture of Columbia, Missouri, they probably think of the six majestic columns. If you think of Fulton you might get a mental image of Winston Churchill's statue and the Berlin Wall. If you say St. Joseph, many would automatically think of the action statue of the pony express rider on that bounding horse.

Diamond, Missouri has the famous statue of George Washington Carver and Kansas City has the wonderful statue of the Indian looking into the distant field of skyscrapers. Of course in Independence people would think of the Truman Presidential Library. Jefferson City is filled with monuments and statues of Famous Missourians.

Hannibal is an unusual one. Your first mental picture of Hannibal is probably of the little white house with the adjoining whitewashed fence.

Sports fans or even drivers on the interstates might think of stadiums when you say the name of a city. Driving though St. Louis on any of three interstates you will see the new Busch Stadium. There is nothing like driving along on I-70 and seeing the two stadiums in Kansas City. Arrowhead Stadium is a historic and beautiful place and right beside it sits the home of the Royals which may be the prettiest little ballpark in America.

Now here's one that many people don't know about. One Missouri city has more fountains than any other American city. In fact only one city in the world has more fountains than Kansas City. Rome has the most fountains and Kansas City, Missouri is a close second.

In fact many of Rome's fountains are just some little things left over from the days of the Roman Empire. The aqueducts brought water to Rome and then pipes carried the water to many public places for the use of the citizens. These "fountains" still exist in many places and they consist of a mound or pillar of concrete with a pipe inside. The little pipe sticks out and water flows from it. The water from these "fountains" is good and clean. They are still used as drinking fountains or to fill water bottles. I just don't think that most Americans would consider them to be real fountains.

The Fountains in Kansas City on the other hand are beautiful objects with sculptures and fascinating sprays, jets, trickles and flows of water. They are usually lighted and objects of beauty. Those lucky enough to have seen the fountains at Branson know that city also has some "braggin' rights" for its fountains which show water formations and colors set to music.

Forty Five: Wildlife Then and Now

When you think of animals in the Midwest, a great variety probably comes to mind. Of course we have deer, turkey, coyotes, squirrels, bobcats, and bears. Now we even have a few mountain lions returning back along the Missouri and its tributaries. There are some buffalo and elk still in the state but not in the vast numbers that were here at one time.

Other animals were here also in the distant past. Skulls and skeletal remains of what people call saber-tooth tigers, are sometimes found in our caves and elsewhere. They weren't really tigers but that name is how they are known. It's hard to imagine these fierce predators prowling our hillsides or using our caves for dens but the proof is all around us.

Mammoths and mastodons were here also. In fact it was probably because of these large mammals that the first people arrived. They were hunters who followed the herds of these giant elephant-like creatures in much the same way that plains Indians followed the herds of bison in later centuries. The large size of the mammoth or mastodon was no match for the large brain of the human. The hunters had spears, arrows, and a weapon-enhancer called an axolotl and, most important, fire. With these they could drive a herd to and over a bluff. Within minutes they had enough meat and supplies to last a village for months.

There was also a prehistoric giant bison which looked much like our modern day buffalo but a lot bigger. It too was hunted by the early native Americans.

One of the strangest and most impressive of the early animals was the Giant Ground Sloth. This lumbering furry creature was about the size of a modern elephant and weighed about 5 tons. It slowly made its way around the landscape eating leaves from the lower branches of trees. There is some good evidence that its hide was so thick and tough that predators could hardly bite it and arrows probably could not pierce it.

In even earlier times fish and underwater creatures abounded because this was the bottom of a prehistoric sea. In fact, the limestone which makes the bedrock of the state was formed at the bottom of the sea. Then a great uplifting occurred and the land emerged. This is why Missouri has an official state fossil, the crinoid, which is a little sea creature.

The best place to see the early creatures including the mastodon, giant ground sloth, and the saber tooth cat is at a state park. Mastodon State Park is located right on Interstate 55 at Imperial just south of St. Louis. You can even visit the dig site where the various bones were found! It's a great place to see tails from the Heartland, and skulls and other parts too.

Missouri's Present Capitol
Jefferson City

Forty Six: Missouri's Many Capitols

We've all seen the beautiful white building which serves as the state's capitol and we know that it is located on that bluff in Jefferson City. However, that has not always been our capital. In fact Missouri has had four different buildings in two different cities. That's if you don't count the two locations in St. Louis where the government met during its earliest days.

We would probably have to say that the very first capital city was the little French town of St. Charles. On the main street of that town the legislature picked a building which would serve as a meeting place for both the Senate and the House. It was understood that this would only be a temporary setting because the state constitution called for the capital to be in the center of the state and near the confluence of the Missouri and

Osage Rivers. Fittingly, now the street in St. Charles where this building is located is named First Capital Drive. The building itself is owned by the state and open to the public.

To bring the state into agreement with its own constitution a decision was made to locate the new capital to a tiny village with about six homes on a bluff overlooking the Missouri River. It was named in honor of Thomas Jefferson who had brought us into the United States a few years earlier. Daniel Boone's son, Daniel Morgan Boone laid out the street plan. The first beautiful Capitol building was built during 1823 to 1826. It can be seen in drawings and paintings of the day. Just eleven years later a mysterious fire destroyed the entire building. One rumor has it that a careless legislator was smoking a cigar in the library. His cigar may have ignited some papers and started the entire blaze.

A new and improved building was erected and ready for use in 1840. This second building on the same location served until 1911 when it also was destroyed by fire. It seems that this time a bolt of lightning caused the blaze.

The present building was first occupied in 1917. It was magnificent at the time and has been improved over the years since that time. The Grand Stairway is 30 feet wide and extends from the first floor all the way to the third. From the stairway's east wall to the west wall it measures 65 feet. The stairway entrance is through a bronze front door which measures 13 feet by 18 feet. This door still holds the record as the largest bronze door since the days of the Roman Empire.

Statues abound inside the capital and out. Of course Jefferson is there as well as statues representing the Mother of the Waters and the Father of the Waters which themselves represent the Mississippi and Missouri Rivers. Statues and busts are located throughout the building representing famous Missourians from Sacajawea Lewis, Clark, and Boone to television personalities and astronauts.

The artwork alone makes the free tour of this building a worthwhile trip. Thomas Hart Benton and others have created murals and paintings here which are beyond monetary value. The most important and most valuable mural by Benton is in the House Lounge. It depicts the entire history of Missouri to the time of its painting. At first, not everyone appreciated the depictions. One legislator tried to sneak in at night with a paint roller and blue paint. He would have destroyed a treasure worth many millions of dollars!

Security requires that you make arrangements in advance but you will be doing yourself a great favor by visiting what is our fourth capitol building in our second capital city.

Forty Seven: War Between the States

When you think of the War Between the States, what states come to mind? Most people think of states in the southeast but those people only know part of the story. Virginia, the capital of the Confederacy, had more battles within her borders than any other state. Missouri, however, was second. Missouri had 1106 battles and skirmishes just during the years 1861-1865. Missouri sent 119,111 volunteers to the war which was, in proportion to her population, more than any other state. Approximately 27,000 Missourians were killed during the Civil War.

Of course, the war began in Missouri a full ten years before what many call the first battle of the Civil War at Fort Sumter. Missouri and Kansas each had free-soil advocates and slavery advocates who battled, fought in guerrilla battles, and burned the cities of Carthage and Nevada in Missouri as well as Lawrence in Kansas. This fighting was done in large part by a group called Jayhawks from Kansas and Quantril's Raiders or Bushwhackers from Missouri.

A demilitarized zone was created along the border and many atrocities were committed in this zone by both sides as well as by the US Army. One elderly lady told a story of growing up during those years. Where our families might have fire drills or drills for earthquakes or tornadoes, they had drills preparing for attacking marauders. The children were to crawl to a small clearing in the middle of their wheat field and hide there until their parents came for them. It's hard to imagine growing up in a setting like that!

Battles were fought all over the state with the biggest being near Springfield at the Battle of Wilson's Creek. Wilson's Creek was the largest battle west of the Mississippi. This was a strange event in many ways. General Nathanial Lyons had earlier taken over Jefferson City and ousted the elected government even though Missouri didn't secede from the Union. People were so afraid of this self-righteous mad man that they fought to defend the state from Gen. Lyons. As a result, Wilson's Creek was fought with a strange assortment of southern soldiers from Missouri, Arkansas, and Louisiana teamed up northern units against Gen. Lyons and his troops.

Since the forces were just being pulled together at the beginning of the war, most did not have uniforms. They identified members of their own units by red bandanas tied around their arms, white shirts or whatever else they could think of. One unit on its way to the battle was walking along for miles talking with another unit going the same direction on the other side of the road. Eventually someone figured out that they were on opposite sides and a sharp officer pulled his men off through a field to keep them from a surprise attack and hand-to-hand fighting. The temporary southern conglomerate defeated Lyons' army and Lyons himself was killed. With this, the northern units went back to fighting for the north and Sterling Price continued with his southern troops for a long and rigorous campaign lasting 3 months and covering over 1,500 miles across Missouri.

The largest federal hospital in the US was at Jefferson Barracks in St. Louis. They had over 3,000 beds with patients coming from as far away as Vicksburg, MS. Stationed at Jefferson Barracks were such notables as U.S. Grant, William Tecumseh Sherman, Braxton Bragg, and many more. St. Louis-built Gunboats keeping the Mississippi open were an important but often overlooked part of the war in Mid-America.

Local historians all over the state can take you to places where skirmishes were fought or where sad events happened. Just ask – In Missouri, history is all around us.

Forty Eight: Our Greatest Disaster

Just west of Hermann a bridge had to be constructed across the wide mouth of the Gasconade River. With it, the Pacific Railroad could jump its biggest obstacle in the expansion westward. Then came the day when the bridge was complete and tracks actually connected St. Louis with the state capital. It was truly a day to remember. November 1, 1855 brought a cold wintry rain to St. Louis but the dignitaries in the railroad cars were warm, dry, and comfortable. This was certainly a wonderful way to travel.

The mayor of St. Louis and all of the City Council was on board, the National Guard Band was there, a military unit, state and county officers, representatives from other railroads, and many high ranking business leaders and professionals. The band played music as they traveled and drinks were served all around. At Hermann, the train stopped and a fifteenth car was added with dignitaries from Hermann and the surrounding area. Another band of musicians also boarded the train at Hermann and another company of uniformed soldiers.

At the Gasconade River everyone planned to get off the train and look at the impressive new bridge which stretched 760 feet across the river. However the train was running a little late and the Governor and more dignitaries were waiting for a ceremony in Jefferson City. So, the train hurried onward through the cold November rain.

At least one engineer had complained that the temporary wooden trestles were not sufficient for a large, fast-moving train. But the executives had made the decision not to wait the extra months to complete the final structure of the bridge. That decision turned out to be a fatal mistake. As the engine crossed the first trestle, the engineer felt the tracks giving way and he yelled, "We're falling!" It was too late for him to do anything else.

The train fell 36 feet into the cold waters below. The car from Hermann somehow stayed on the tracks on the east bank. The engine, tender, and seven cars fell through the broken timbers. All of the others were pulled rolling down the river bank and into the water.

As the rain intensified, the engine lay steaming and hissing halfway under water, those people left alive were screaming for help and those who were able did their best to free others from the wreckage and stop their bleeding. The mangled and bleeding survivors were carried to some nearby shanties and many were moved to a hotel in Hermann which was converted into a makeshift hospital. Over thirty were killed in those first minutes and hundreds had serious injuries. Almost everyone suffered some sort of injury and they all suffered from exposure.

The rain didn't stop. All through the next day it continued as a hospital train arrived from St. Louis and replacement soldiers helped to carry the bodies of the dead to freight cars and those still alive were taken to passenger cars.

This rescue train immediately left for St. Louis but when it arrived at Boeuf Creek in Franklin County, it was raging out of its banks and they could go no further. This bridge also seemed in danger of failure.

A plan emerged for those who were able, to walk across the bridge, and the hospital cars would keep the most seriously injured at that location.

For those already across, the cars would be pushed across one at a time. Then the locomotive would be brought by itself. As the very first car was pushed onto the bridge this second bridge collapsed. Another train arrived to take the less injured people to Washington, Missouri, ferryboats did the rest and eventually the ordeal ended and the worst railroad disaster in Missouri's history was over.

Forty Nine: One Room Schools

Those of us who began our education in one-room schools tend to forget that not everyone shares those memories. Children in those schools had almost none of the wonderful advantages that today's children enjoy and yet, everyone seems to have such rich and pleasant memories of the experience.

In spite of what Grandfather told you, he probably did not have to walk ten miles each way going to and from schools. He probably did not have to walk uphill both ways either. However, many did walk great distances using shortcuts through the woods and balancing on slippery logs as they crossed swollen streams. The lucky ones lived far enough away that they were allowed to ride a horse to school. Later many children got to ride in the family car or pickup truck. This was a vast improvement because you not only stayed dry on rainy days but you stayed warm on cold days.

Many country schools opened in September and then closed just before Christmas. They would remain closed during the winter months and open again from early March through early May. Boys would often have to miss those weeks in April and May because they were needed for plowing and planting. These were primitive places where people would write with chalk on slates. In other words they would drag one rock across another to write their lessons.

Teachers were often eighth grade graduates who had attended a short course at a Normal School. These Normal Schools were teacher-training institutions and were located in many places around the state. Some of them are now state universities in the Midwestern states. Since boys got to attend less time each year, it took them longer to get through school and they were sometimes older than their teachers. It wasn't unheard of for teachers and students to be married after graduation.

These older boys could sometimes be a problem for their younger teachers. They would take pride in "running a teacher off" as a proof of their dubious manhood. In the county where I grew up there was a one-armed war veteran who would sometimes be called in to set these older boys straight. He would try to get them back in line and they would challenge his authority or ability and this kindest and most gentle of men would give them a beating. Soon he would announce that a new teacher would be coming and that everyone should treat her with respect so he (the veteran) wouldn't need to be invited back again.

Some teachers were more considerate than others. In my county, Morris Hill was one of those. He would arrive at school each morning in time to start the fire in the pot-bellied stove so the school would be nice and warm for the students. On top of the stove he would put a pot of beans to cook through the day so the children would have a warm lunch on those cold days.

Smaller schools would only admit students every other year so if you were six this year, you could start first grade but there would be no class starting next year so next year's six-year-old would have to wait until he was seven. That way the teacher would only have to prepare lessons for four groups of children instead of eight. Of course, with Math, Reading, Language, and Spelling, that was still 80 lessons to prepare each week. The older children might also have classes like Science or Civics.

The Heartland is full of well-preserved "school houses" and each uniquely reflects its community. There is something to be learned every time you stop and visit one of these important relics of our past. Why not do that soon?

Fifty: Rosemary's Ride to School

A lady I knew told me this story of her childhood on the Prairie in North Missouri. Her name was Rosemary and she attended elementary school in Jamesport. Now Rosemary was a lucky girl for many reasons. She got to go to school, she lived far enough away that she got to ride a horse to school, and her parents were protective of her.

It's hard for us to remember a time when weather forecasting wasn't very accurate and radio stations were few and far between. That was the situation however, as Rosemary got ready for school. Her father, Sam Thompson, was saddling her horse and watching the sky. The clouds were low and thick but there were just flurries swirling and nothing seemed out of the ordinary. Just being cautious, Sam checked to be sure that Rosemary was bundled up with plenty of layers and then he did something unusual. He took a large wool blanket and cut a split in the middle. He placed this over his daughter's head so it fell down and gave her an extra layer of warmth and it held the warmth of the horse's body as well.

As instructed, Rosemary took the shortcut to school and traveled right down the railroad tracks. She hadn't been gone for long when the flurries turned to big wet feathery flakes and then the wind picked up. Before long the wind was blowing an even heavier snowfall. Soon the flakes were blowing sideways and she couldn't see even the ears of her horse. She was caught in a blizzard and white-out conditions.

She trusted the horse and, sure enough, the horse kept moving somehow sensing where they were. Then the horse balked and stopped. There they sat not being able to see anything and having no idea where they were.

Soon after Rosemary left home Sam realized what the situation was and he saddled up and went after her. A neighbor tending his stock saw Sam and asked where he was going. The neighbor joined the rescue. By the time they got to the tracks, they couldn't see where they going. They dismounted and grabbed their extra blankets and began walking down the tracks. They managed to do this by sliding the outside of one foot along the inside of a track. This was all that kept them on course. The men kept calling to Rosemary and finally they heard a welcome reply.

There, in the middle of the tracks, in the middle of who-knew-where, they decided to huddle down and wait for the storm to let up. They hoped to be able to hear a train before it arrived and hoped that they could count on the horse to help with that. As they sat in the blind white cold they talked about what they would like to do when the storm subsided. Rosemary wanted a big mug of cocoa. Sam said he would like plenty of hot coffee and the neighbor said he had missed breakfast and would like a steaming bowl of stew.

No trains came and finally the storm ended. At last they could see and they realized that they were just a few feet away from a large white farmhouse. And what do you suppose their friendly neighbors had just concocted? Beef stew! Coffee and cocoa were easy additions and the scariest trip to school ended in the warm kitchen of a prairie farmhouse.

Fifty One: The Missouri-Kansas Rivalry

People living on the eastern side of Missouri often don't get it. I'm talking about the rivalry between the sports teams from Missouri and Kansas. Probably people in the west don't understand what happens with the St. Louis Cardinals and the Chicago Cubs either but that Missouri-Kansas thing is something very special.

The rivalry started way back in 1854 before either college even had sports teams. As a matter of fact, the University of Kansas itself didn't even exist in 1854. But in that year, a border war erupted between the two states. It led to John Brown and his followers hacking five Missourians to death with swords, the destruction of two cities in Missouri and one in Kansas, the deaths of over 300 Missouri women who were being held captive, and many more atrocities.

Thank goodness the border war is fought now with footballs and basketballs instead of bullets! We also are no longer trying to exact revenge for the past. I'm just trying to emphasize the depth of feeling and the long history of this rivalry. In fact the games between these two teams are so full of competitiveness and emotion that they are often the best games of the year. It is all done in the best spirit. This is something that the Cardinals-Cubs rivalry participants would understand. The teasing and joking is all done in the best of fun.

In the earliest years of the Missouri-Kansas games they were almost always played in Kansas City. Once they played in St. Joseph but K.C. was the logical place for such an important game and for the convenience of all alumni. Then the conference and the NCAA decided that all games should be played on campus. The MU-KU game became the final climax game of each football season. This meant that cold weather was often a feature of the game. At one game in the 1960s, it was so cold that Marchin' Mizzou's instruments froze. The woodwinds' cork pads froze tight and the brass slides and valves were frozen in place. At halftime the drums played on their rims to keep the volume down and the other musicians just sang their parts as they performed. They earned a huge ovation.

In 1911 the football game was to be played in Columbia and Athletic Director, Chester Brewer, invited all MU alumni to "come home" and support the team for this big game. A record crowd of 9000 alumni showed up and were greeted with a spirit rally and a parade. It became an annual tradition at Mizzou and at every college and high school in the nation. Indeed that game in 1911 was the nations' very first homecoming.

The rivalry is not all fun and games for the coaches. Several in recent memory could routinely beat football power schools but lost their jobs because they couldn't beat Kansas. One year Mizzou's record was 10 wins and 1 loss. Would you like to guess who they lost to? In 2007 Missouri and Kansas met to see which team would be ranked number one in the nation. Prior to that game their record against each other was Missouri 53 wins, Kansas 53 wins, and 9 games had ended in ties. Oh, yes, Missouri did win that game in 2007.

Fifty Two: Environmental Successes

I guess that it's the job of the environmentalists to point with alarm at what's all around us. I suppose they are trying to shock us or worry us into action. Well, I'm kind of tired of it.

It's not that we shouldn't keep trying to make the world a better place. That's not it at all. Don't you like the way that scout groups and others always try to leave a campsite better than it was when they arrived? I think we should all try to be that way. As an amateur historian I have an ever-deepening appreciation for the settlers who came here and worked so hard to leave things better for their children and grand-children than what they had for themselves. Sometimes now we might disagree about what "better" really is but those old-timers did whatever they could to make their lands, their businesses, and their homes better for the next generation.

I think that we are leaving our environment better for the next generations than what we had ourselves. When I grew up in the Ozarks I lived about eight miles from the nearest city and the land around our 120 acres was partially farmed but mostly wild. Even so, I never saw a deer in the wild until I was in my late 20s and that was in St. Louis County. I had to wait a while longer before I got to see my first wild turkey. Now both are plentiful.

Driving from the Ozarks toward St. Louis or Kansas City was always a little creepy because of the brown haze which hung over those places. It was visible long before you got near any tall buildings or even the suburbs. On those same trips we would cross over rivers which were brown with runoff soil, herbicides, and pesticides. Some were capped with white fluffy mounds of fish-killing phosphates. Bennett Spring was the only stream I ever saw with clean water. All that is improved to an amazing degree!

Lady Bird Johnson made us all aware of litterbugs and Missourians and others responded. The roadsides used to be deep with litter of all kinds. Now, no one with any pride would throw litter from their cars.

Other wildlife has been making a comeback also. There have been enough bears in Missouri that we have had a bear hunting season for many years now. My science teacher years ago told us that if we could get the deer population up, that certain predators like wolves and mountain lions would reappear also. The populations of coyotes and coy dogs have grown so fast that I'm not sure about those wolves but it's abundantly clear that mountain lions are returning to the state coming from the west along the Missouri River and its tributaries.

So, come on environmentalists. Give us a break. We recognized the problems, acted on them, and now let's recognize the successes. Go ahead and do your job of making us aware but I think that right now, we all deserve a round of applause and a heartfelt, "Thank you."

Fifty Three: Rocks and Minerals

I suppose that every state has rocks beneath the soil but in Missouri it's those rocks which shaped the development of our state. Much of the state is built on a bedrock of limestone. This comes from an ancient seafloor which and contains the fossils from that ocean which originally covered the Midwest. The limestone provides rich nutrients for grasses which covered the prairie in the north and west. This natural grassland also provides great grazing land now as well as a great place to grow newer grasses such as corn and wheat.

To many Missouri is The Cave State. Of course this is only true because water running through cracks and fissures in the limestone gradually eat away the rock until large openings are formed. In some of the best caves, the water also leaves beautiful mineral deposits. Sometimes the water courses underground for a great distance and then comes out of the limestone at places like Bennett Spring, Big Spring, Alley Spring, and Meramec Springs State Parks.

Of course we can't overlook that this limestone and limestone gravel provide cheap building material for roads and many buildings. The best quality limestone comes from the area around Carthage and is known as Carthage Marble. It is of such quality that many people look at limestone buildings like our state capitol and think that it is actually made of marble.

There are strange sights to be seen across the northern half of Missouri. Almost everything north of the Missouri River is built on limestone. Yet, in many fields and parks there can be found large, round, scarred rocks of all kinds. Sometimes the nearest similar rocks are as far away a Minnesota. What are they? They are called glacial erratics and were carried here by the massive sheets of ice which covered all of north Missouri in the last Ice Age. As the glaciers melted away, they left these rocks behind.

In the southeastern part of the state they have less limestone and more granite. This beautiful pink granite is quarried for monuments, buildings, and more. We can see them in places like the Johnson Shut-Ins and Elephant Rocks State Parks. Where limestone wears away easily with moving water, granite does not. Limestone valleys are broad and wide. Granite valleys are narrow and deep. This is why the Shut-Ins are so swift and why the St. Francois River has Olympic quality stretches of white water. This part of the state also is the home to one of America's premier mining schools, the Missouri University of Science and Technology at Rolla.

Finally, let's not forget that the first European and African settlers who came to Missouri came here for our rocks. The first were lead miners and Missouri does have the largest lead belt in the world. Then these same miners discovered great quantities of iron there in that same area which we now call the Mineral Area.

The next time you pass through Ironton, Leadwood, Graniteville, or Old Mines, give a thought to how these names were chosen. They're a part of who we are.

Fifty Four: Stage Coaches

When I think of stagecoaches I get all sorts of mixed feelings. It's hard to know what is fact and what is Hollywood. The more I learned about stagecoaches and their part in Missouri's history, the more I realized how important they were and just how little we all know about them today.

The first stagecoach in Missouri seems to have been one which ran a route from St. Louis to Franklin, Missouri in 1820. Missouri was not yet a state at this point and Franklin (near Boonville) was about as far west as anything at that time. These coaches became increasingly popular forms of transportation with many routes just running from ferry boat landings to small towns in St. Louis County. They were the taxi cabs or city busses of their day.

The more traditional view of stagecoaches is of the kind depicted in movies where the coach carries passengers across vast expanses between small towns. There were plenty of these too. The truth, however is that passengers helped to pay the bills but the real money came from carrying the US Mail. The famous Butterfield stage coach was really named the Butterfield Overland Mail Company. This line began in 1858 and carried the mail, some parcels, and passengers from St. Louis to California. Of course the coaches stopped at many places along the way. In addition to St. Louis, important Missouri stage stops included Tipton, Warsaw, Wheatland, Elkton, Bolivar, Brighton, Springfield, Clever, and Cassville.

In order to get paid the $600,000 for taking mail twice a week from St. Louis to San Francisco, a trip of 2,812 miles, the trip had to be made in 25 days or less. Without good roads, this was not an easy matter. The average speed was eight miles per hour. It is interesting to know that this 25 day target was never ever missed.

Springfield was an important place on the route because it was here that the passengers, parcels, and mail were all switched from the 3,000 pound Concord stage to a Celerity Wagon. This was an open-sided vehicle which was thought to be better suited to the heat of the Southwest. It was slung on leather straps rather than springs and it allowed room inside for nine passengers (allowing 15 inches per person) and twelve more people were allowed to ride on top. At night the two seats and one bench all folded together to make one large leather bed. Those bouncing on top didn't have a bed. They would do well to just stay on board. Mules often replaced horses at Springfield also. Because of this, the stage line got the nickname of the "Jackass Mail."

As I said, this business was about the mail and not about passengers. Once they left Missouri there were no such niceties as fresh food and often no plates or cups for the food which was there. One traveler described his meal at a stagecoach stop as coffee, shortcake, beef jerky and whole onions. The fare from St. Louis to San Francisco was $200 plus 75 cents to a dollar per meal. Each person was allowed 40 pounds of luggage but it had to be carried on their lap. Mail pouches were under their feet on the floor of the stage.

Even with the coming of railroads, the stage coach continued to be the best method of travel between small communities. It was the motor bus which finally replaced stage coaches in about 1915. With their passing, an important part of our past had become history.

1950s Style Bicycle

Fifty Five: Old Time Bicycles

Fifty or sixty years ago bicycles were big sturdy things. They were made to be ridden year after year after year. The youngsters who rode them were pretty sturdy too. The legs develop a lot of strength and stamina from hours of peddling. This peddling was often to get you to a place where you could swim, race, play ball or any number of other things. The bikes were sturdy and they made us sturdy.

In the little Missouri town where I grew up there was a way to equip you bikes too. Now this may be something common to lots of places but I can't speak about lots of places. In my town most boys had a baseball glove hung on the handlebars by slipping one handlebar through the strap which goes across the back of the glove.

Over the back fender we had a carrier. It was supposed to be a seat but, since everyone had a bike of their own, there was no need to carry a second person on a bike. Instead these carriers usually had a baseball bat tied to one side and a rod & reel tied to the other side. A small fishing tackle box would sit on the carrier just under the "driver's" seat.

Finally there was a basket fastened over the front fender. In this we could carry our school books, a basketball, lunch, a jacket, a swimsuit, or whatever else might be needed. We were prepared for anything! If you had streamers and mirrors on your handlebars, you were not only prepared but you were really stylin'.

Of course there were days when we had to make noise and get noticed. At these times we would use a clothespin to hold playing cards in the spokes and we had a motor. An even better motor could be had by tying a balloon on the fender's crossbar and letting the spokes thump it in a fast or slow roar. Some kids even had a siren which could be pulled with a string up against the wheel. These sirens would actually bring people to their doors and windows. We were really getting noticed then!

Now I don't know about where you lived but, where I lived the boys would earn and save money so they could by automobile hood ornaments to put on their front bicycle fenders. Of course it looked both beautiful and impressive but it was a risky business. I once put a gigantic chrome swan on the front fender of my Schwinn. I had a wreck that very first day and I'll never forget the look on the faces of my parents when they saw my brand new red bike with a huge ragged hole torn in the front fender.

We also took what we called bicycle hikes. We would load up for the day and take off to see a plane wreck, a caboose, a longhorn, or whatever else the countryside had to offer. One favorite destination was a tall barn with lofts on both sides and a rope for swinging from one loft to the other. Many pirate ships were boarded in that barn!

This may sound silly to some but I firmly believe that the independence and self-reliance gained from those days peddling our bikes gave us what we needed to tackle the world and succeed as adults. My friends and I owe our parents many thanks for allowing us that freedom and we owe the people of rural Missouri for making us safe.

Fifty Six: After the James Gang

We've all heard about the exploits of Frank and Jesse James and their cousins the Youngers. They never were Robin Hoods but they were very popular for various reasons. For one thing they shared a common misery with many people in western Missouri. The Missourians had been oppressed for years by bankers, railroads, and the US Army. These are the very targets of most of the James Gang's activities. People may not have liked the robberies and shootings but they sure enjoyed seeing their oppressors get a black eye.

Most people know now that both Frank and Jesse rode with Quantril's Raiders and that Frank served with Gen. Sterling Price during the Civil War. Afterwards they continued to strike out at targets of all kinds. They basically invented train robberies and accepted advertisements about "un-robbable" banks as personal challenges. Thanks to Frank, Jesse and their cousins, the Youngers, Missouri's nickname at the time was "The Outlaw State."

At one point Jesse decided to settle down and assumed the identity of a Mr. Howard but, In St. Joseph, a friend shot him in the back in order to claim a reward. This left only brother, Frank who likewise wanted to live a more peaceful life.

Five months after the murder of Jesse, Frank arrived in Jefferson City to keep an appointment with Governor Crittenden. He put his gun in the governor's hands and said:

*I have been hunted for 21 years, have literally lived in the saddle,
have never known a day of perfect peace. It was one long,
anxious, inexorable, eternal vigil. Governor, I haven't let another
man touch my gun since 1861.*

With that he surrendered to the authority of the state. He was tried for his part in two robberies, one at the bank in Gallatin, MO and one for a train robbery at Winston, MO. He was acquitted on both of those charges. Next he went to Alabama and stood trial for the robbery of a U.S. Army payroll. No Alabama jury would blame him for that!

In his last thirty years he held many jobs. He was a shoe salesman and then a theater guard in St. Louis. Then he got a better job with A.T. & T. as a telegraph operator in St. Joseph. Then he and his cousin, Cole Younger, took up the lecture circuit. Frank was very well-educated for the time and was well-known as an authority on the works of William Shakespeare so this lecturing and public speaking suited him well. Then an old friend from Missouri hired him as the betting commissioner at a race track in New Orleans. Frank James, of all people, as the betting commissioner! Does that sound like putting a rat in charge of the cheese? But apparently he did a good job and worked there until he retired back to his family farm near Liberty, Missouri. There he supplemented his income by giving tours to tourists for 25 cents each.

This man who put the "wild" in wild west died there where he had spent his boyhood on February 18, 1915.

**Dr. David C. Ashley, Missouri Western State U.
Ascending from Coffin Cave, Laclede County**

Fifty Seven: Caves and Sinkholes

Of course Missouri is known to many as "The Cave State" because it has over 7,000 caves. The limestone bedrock of the state and the plentiful rainfall are what's needed for our abundance of caves. This water runoff is also acidic in the Ozarks because rain and snowmelt leach down through leaves and pine needles. This turns the water into a mild tannic acid.

Everyone knows about those caves which have been commercially developed. They are fascinating and often beautiful. Some of the best are Meramec Caverns, Crystal Cave, Bridal Cave, Fantastic Caverns, Tom Sawyer's Cave, and Marvel Cave. Two great historic caves are now state parks. Graham Cave and Onondaga Cave are accessible from Interstate 70 and Interstate 44 and well worth the visit.

One of my favorite cave-related features is sinkholes. Sinkholes happen when the roof of a cave collapses. With time these can actually be hard to see. Some are so large that they actually look like a valley. Others get completely covered with tall trees and aren't visible even from the air. Some sinkholes which occur on flatland can even be hard to recognize. The water which flowed through and formed the cave can continue to flow into the depression and create a wonderful spring-fed pond. The town where I grew up began as Wyota, an Osage Village at the side of a sinkhole. The Osage gave a spiritual importance to that particular sinkhole.

A high school friend, George Kastler, went all the way to the National Science Fair by mapping and describing the caves in our county. He found more than a hundred at that time. One, Coffin Cave, has the largest group of hibernating Gray Bats in the state. George, by the way, is now the Chief Naturalist for Missouri's Parks Department. He discovered that anyone with an interest can find wonderful things all around us in Missouri. There are lots of wonderful things in Perry County. They have about 7,000 caves!

Sometimes we think so much about cave formations and temperatures that we overlook the animals who dwell underground. Missouri's caves have many kinds of blind white creatures like cavefish, crayfish, millipedes, and spiders. These critters live their entire lives underground. Other animals just love to use caves on a part-time basis. Bats, for instance, hunt at night then sleep in caves during the day. Cave salamanders, sculpin and springfish are good examples of these cave users. Others who use caves regularly include mice, bears, raccoons, wildcats, frogs, and crickets.

Indians used the controlled climate and protected environment of caves for many purposes. Because of this there are still many Indian artifacts to be found. The special nature of caves also provided special advantages for pioneers. One of the most historic places in the state is the cave near St. Albans which was used by Indians, then by river pirates, and later by tavern owners dealing with the mountain men as they returned with their pelts. Meriwether Lewis fell 200 feet from this cave and almost died just as they started their expedition. Missouri's caves hold many stories. To experience Missouri's wild caves, be sure to get information first from the Missouri Geologic Survey in Rolla.

Fifty Eight: Ozarks Sayings

Good Ozarks sayings give you something to chew on for a while. The point doesn't just jump out at you. It's on levels and comes back at you after you've heard it. One Ozark philosopher said, "He'd climb a tree to tell a lie when truth would do on the ground." Haven't you known people who just enjoyed the lie? They would rather put one over on you than share plane old talk. It may be harder to do but, to them, it's worth it.

Another good saying came one day as a group of farmers sat in front of Cackle Hatchery while their wives were getting groceries in Barnes Market. A man we'll call Mr. Gibson arrived in a beautiful new pickup truck. He was a little too proud of his purchase and his pride really did turn into bragging. As he left, on old-timer spit into a can and quietly said, "I know fer fact, all them Gibson boys was born necked." That's the way it is in rural communities. Everybody is on pretty much the same level because, if you go back far enough, we're all born necked.

This also reminds me of the comment my best friend made about me when I was a boy. He said, "If he <u>had</u> a little brain, he'd have it in his hand a-playin' with it." That's another thing about Ozark humor – It teases and pokes fun at you. It levels the playing field and keeps things friendly.

Back in 1976, in Lebanon High School's Bittersweet Magazine, Jenny Kelso collected some good sayings which also give you something to chew on after you first hear them. Here are a few of the good ones that Jenny gathered.

"I wish I was a rich man's dog and my owner didn't have any cattle." That guy would have to be about as lazy as the one who was said to be, "too lazy to say 'sooey' if the hogs was eatin' him up.

I have mixed feelings about the man who drawled, "The ole cow stepped on my foot. It sure felt good when she got off."

People in the Ozarks get just as busy as the rest of us. In fact one was said to be, "...busy as a stump-tailed cow in fly time." Now there's a mental picture! Speaking of a mental picture, how about the person who was as, "Nervous as a porcupine in a balloon factory."

How flattered would you feel if someone said, "He takes to you like a hog after persimmons?" How flattered would you feel if someone said that you are, "Cooler than the center of a cucumber?"

One last quote from Jenny – an old man is said to have stated, "I don't know the exact date I was born. I know it was tater time. But I don't know if it was diggin' or plantin'."

Finally I want to point out that to say these things correctly in the Ozark tongue, you have to smile a broad smile and remember that, in the Ozarks, there are only two vowels. They are a "long O" and a "long A." For instance, when commenting on a pretty girl's appearance, you say, "Shay shore is a swaat thang."

Fifty Nine: Kewpie Dolls

We've all seen "must have" toys such as Tickle-Me Elmo, Game Boy, and more. Do you remember those loveable but ugly little Cabbage Patch Kids? This is not, however, a new phenomenon. A hundred years ago every child wanted Teddy Bears, Kewpie Dolls, and Billikens. Teddy Bears are still popular and Billikens have become the mascot for St. Louis University, but what are Kewpies?

We've all heard of Cupid. We all know that Cupid can get people in trouble. Of course it's the best kind of trouble but when we start doing things because of our emotions instead of logic we might need help. Well, for about a century now, help has been here. The help was brought to us by Rose O'Neill of Branson, Missouri. Her life centered around Bonniebrook, her family's home near Branson. She first came there in 1896 and from there traveled the world.

Ms. O'Neill introduced us to her creations, the Kewpie dolls. The Kewpies were to bring us luck and to help perform good deeds in funny ways. This author and Illustrator was a champion of equal rights for women and she wrote for women's magazines like the Ladies Home Journal. The actions of the Kewpies were an early version of what today we would call comic strips. Some were printed on the front and back of a page so they could be cut out and used for paper dolls.

It was in 1909 that she developed the concept of these little helpers and asked an artist friend to help her put her ideas on paper. They were instantly popular. Kewpies were used to help create interest and make points in favor of women's rights as they appeared in many women's magazines. Little dolls were made first of bisque and then celluloid. Within 30 years they grew steadily to become a worldwide phenomenon. Some folks will remember Kewpie coloring books, cups, plates, curios, poetry, and more.

The two most famous Kewpies may have been 1939 creations. One was buried in a time capsule at the New York World's Fair to show future generations what life was like at that time. The other was given to Anne Franke as she hid in the attic in Amsterdam. It was her gift for St. Nicholas Day.

One of the strangest parts of the Kewpie story is the places where they have the most staying power. One place is in Japan where they have Kewpie brand mayonnaise. That's right the most popular mayonnaise in Japan is named Kewpie and has a picture of a Kewpie on the front of each container.

The second place with great staying power for the Kewpie is at Hickman High School in Columbia, Missouri. Most football and sports teams are named for ferocious animals or famous warrior groups. Hickman's teams, on the other hand, are called the Kewpies. This doesn't sound quite so funny however when you know that the Hickman football team holds the national record for consecutive wins. After all, Kewpies are supposed to bring good luck and help you, so maybe they are the best mascot of all!

Sixty: Small Schools' Teams

I want to tell you about a day that started me re-thinking my opinion about many things in small schools. I lived in a consolidated district so our small town high school was actually a little larger than average. I was on the basketball team and we wore black and gold uniforms. The day I'm recalling was when I was in the 7th grade.

Our team was wearing our new uniforms for the first time and we were on our way to play at a tiny town nearby. Our new uniforms were silky shiny gold with black numerals and white trim. We had pullover warm-up jackets that zipped part way down the front. Our school mascot was on the jacket. We were cool!

When we got to the gym, we dressed out and began to practice. We noticed immediately that the court was not big enough. It had <u>two</u> center lines! You had to take the ball across both center lines and then could bring it back out beyond the one to play your half-court game. It was very disorienting. Worse yet, when we tried to dribble the ball, it bounced every which way because the floor was so badly warped.

Then out came the home team. They were wearing blue jeans and white tee shirts. That was their uniform. At that point I was feeling so sorry for them I actually wished we could take off our beautiful new uniforms. That was the last time I felt pity because the game got immediately underway.

We played pretty well I think but we just couldn't pull ahead by more than a point or two. The coach called "time out" and we huddled. He pointed out that because of the floor, we couldn't dribble so much. We had to quit playing like individuals and start playing like a team. More passing, more watching for the open man, more teamwork.

To make a long story short, those small town boys taught us a great lesson that night. There were fewer boys in their school from whom to choose a team but they were superior basketball players. Everything we did, they could do better. (Except maybe look good in our uniforms and we really quit caring about that.)

My dad wasn't surprised at all. He pointed out that that little town didn't have enough players to make a football team. They didn't have little league or even a swimming pool. Since they didn't spread their efforts so thin, they got very good at those things which they did do.

This holds true for things other than sports too. Over the years I have seen wonderful things in places like Plato, Malta Bend, Carl Junction, and Laquey, Missouri. Don't know much about them? You would if you or your children ever had to compete against them on History Day, music competitions, Brain Bowl, math contests, sports, Academic Decathlon, or art festivals. They may do fewer things but what they do, they do very well!

One last note – If you go to a small school, the other kids really count on you. They truly need every student to be the best they can be. There is a positive peer pressure to do the best you can in lots of areas or let your friends down. Of course they do well when they compete. School spirit really means something in small schools!

Sixty One: Generals from Missouri

Besides being generals in the army, what do Dwight David Eisenhower, U.S. Grant, Braxton Bragg, Stephen Kearny, and William Tecumseh Sherman have in common? The answer is – Missouri. All of these men were stationed at Jefferson Barracks in St. Louis. Kearny was the first commander there and it was there that he formed the first unit of the U.S. Cavalry. There were many others though they may not be so famous. Robert E. Lee was not stationed at Jefferson Barracks but he did live in St. Louis while he led the effort to control the flow of the Mississippi River and keep it flowing in its channel past the St. Louis levee.

General Grant of course lived at Grant's Farm in St. Louis County and his wife was from a prominent family in that area but Missouri was important to his career for many reasons. He routed Confederate forces in July of 1861 while operating from his headquarters in Monroe City, Missouri. Grant received his commission as Brigadier General later that year at Ironton, Missouri. When he needed gunboats for the Siege of Vicksburg and control of the Mississippi, he called on his St. Louis friend, James Eads. Later his friend from Hannibal, Sam Clemens, would help him in many ways through Grant's final years.

Sterling Price was a great General Officer for the southern side. He seemed able to take a loose coalition of militias and individuals and win battles without sufficient food, clothing, guns, ammunition, tents, or any of the other supplies any army needs. His victories include Wilson's Creek, Lexington, and Pea Ridge.

John J. Pershing was born in Laclede, Missouri. He graduated from high school and took a job teaching in a high school for black students. Then, he found that a free college education is available for young people at the US Military Academy. He was accepted into the Academy. When he graduated and was ready for his first command, someone noticed his previous experience with young black people. He was given command of an all-black military unit and his nickname became Black Jack Pershing. During America's participation in World War I, Pershing was selected to be the Commander of all American troops. This hero earned the rank of Five Star General and was named "General of the Armies." No one other than George Washington had ever held that rank.

Omar Bradley was known as the Soldier's Soldier. He was born In Clark, Missouri. He was most famous for being gentle and kind. Correspondents claim that he never issued orders without saying, "Please." During World War II, Bradley became a five-star-general and was named General of the Armies as Pershing had been in the earlier war. After the war he became the Army Chief of Staff and the Chairman of the Joint Chiefs of Staff. His service spanned Mexican Border service, World War I, World War II, and Korea.

Bradley is known for saying, "Ours is a world of nuclear giants and ethical infants. We know more about war than about peace, more about killing than we know about living." During his great career he never lost his thoughtful Midwestern outlook.

Sixty Two: The Nation's Worst Maritime Disaster

When we think of great maritime disasters, events like the Titanic, or the Edmund Fitzgerald might come to mind. However, neither of these was as bad a disaster as the sinking of the Sultana on the Mississippi River

The War Between the States officially ended on April 9, 1865. On April 14 Lincoln was assassinated. Finding John Wilkes Booth and the trial of Dr. Mudd consumed the public's attention and maybe that is why we haven't heard more about the sinking of the Sultana on the 27th of that same month.

The Sultana was a new ship, only 3 years old. It was fairly large and built to haul cotton down the rivers to market. It's duty had been to carry troops between St. Louis and New Orleans. At this time the mission was much happier. The prisoners had just been released from the hell that was Andersonville Prison and the Sultana was to take them home from where they waited in Vicksburg. As it left New Orleans many soldiers simply climbed on board eager to get back to their homes in the Midwest. The final destination was Jefferson Barracks in St. Louis. Built for a crew of 85 and permitted to carry another 376 passengers, it was soon overwhelmed as thousands crowded on board. No one knows just how many.

At Vicksburg the gaunt malnourished Andersonville veterans were brought aboard in something described as a stampede and the Sultana continued northward. In spite of their misery the men began singing, joking, and eagerly anticipating homes which they previously thought they might never see. They made a scheduled stop at Memphis and headed for Cairo. This was very significant because Cairo was the first stop in Illinois, Kentucky and Ohio were just up the Ohio to the east and Missouri was just across the Mississippi on the west bank. Most of the men would see their home states for the first time in a long time. Cairo was the place where most of the men would disembark.

The Sultana labored upstream. The Mississippi was swollen with the Spring runoff and cold with snowmelt coming down from the Upper Mississippi, Missouri, and Illinois Rivers. Just after midnight on April 27 as the soldiers slept blissfully, it happened.

The boilers exploded. The men were thrown into the icy waters and the swift current. One survivor said that for a minute the river seemed to be a mass of struggling men. But many were too weak to swim at all and even the strongest had almost no chance in that kind of water. A few were able to grasp onto floating debris and dodge the flaming coals which rained all around them. Others were trapped on the wooden boat and burned alive. A captured 10-foot alligator was caged on the boat. One quick-thinking soldier bayoneted the maneater and then rolled the cage overboard and jumped into the water using the wooden cage as a floatation device.

No one knows how many died that night. Estimates range from 1,500 to 1,900. Probably about 1,800 would be a good guess. Either way, this night on the Mississippi River saw the worst maritime disaster in U.S. history.

**The Castle Ruins
Ha Ha Tonka**

Sixty Three: Ha Ha Tonka

Strange as it may seem, when I was a teenager, my friends and I would sometimes sit around at night in an actual castle. More accurately, I should say in castle ruins. Just a few miles from our Missouri homes were the burned-out remains of a huge castle constructed of limestone by Scottish stone masons. As we would sit in the moonlight the stone walls seemed gray and mysterious. They seemed to cast a spell on us that made the drive worthwhile. The castle was most famous for it's tragedies. Caves here were used by robbers and counterfeiters in the earliest days of the area's history.

I'll never forget the one night in this otherworldly place when I heard my first screech owl. It scared the bejeebers out of us! It sounded for all the world like a woman screaming and the best we could do afterwards was to laugh nervously and pretend not to be bothered. Only everyone else was startled – not me of course.

Many will realize that I'm talking about Ha Ha Tonka. The name probably comes from the Osage Indians and means Laughing Waters. In the late 1800s Robert Snyder from Kansas City began purchasing land and eventually owned about 2500 acres. Snyder was somewhat famous for being one of the first automobile owners in the state. Then he hired an architect, a supervisor, and stone masons from Scotland. Construction began in 1905. Then, in 1906 Snyder was killed in an automobile accident. Snyder's sons picked up the project and completed it.

When completed the castle was 3½ stories tall, with a stone stable, nine greenhouses, and an eighty foot water tower. The most impressive part of the castle in the good old days was the great hall. This was also true in Scotland's castles. Even today, it is the most impressive part of the castle ruins. In 1942 disaster came again to the Snyders. Sparks from the gigantic fireplace set the building afire.

In 1978 the property was purchased to serve as a state park. Surprisingly, it wasn't the castle which was so interesting to park authorities. Instead it was the collapsed cave, several intact caves with massive stalagmites, several natural bridges, the Lake of the Ozarks, cliff walls, wildlife, and an unusually beautiful spring with a flow of 49 million gallons per day. There is even a naturally-occurring balanced dolomite rock. The Parks Department has put in about 15 miles of developed trails.

Of course there are many other places to spend enjoyable times in the area. After all, this castle sits above the Lake of the Ozarks. The lake area has something for everyone.

My wife and I have just decided that we're going to visit Ha Ha Tonka. After all, many people claim that this is the jewel of the state's park system. Maybe we'll see you there.

Sixty Four: An Osage Village

Where were the Osage Indians? Who were the Osage Indians? Where are they now? Let's address those questions in reverse order. First, where are they now? Well, they're all around us and they are us. The Osage were so friendly, helpful and compatible with the white settlers that many of them intermarried. The French especially were fond of marrying Osage partners.

The second question of who were they can be answered by the many descriptions left for us by the area's earliest settlers and explorers. The Osage were a distinct nation with their own customs, beliefs, language, and style of living but they were closely related to the Sioux who were their neighbors on the west. They were amazingly tall and good looking. We don't have to take anyone's word for this. Many Osage were painted by George Catlin and the great artists of the Missouri Valley and the west.

Finally, where were they? This is the harder question. Some village sites were identified by settlers and explorers but the very reasons that made them good places for Indian inhabitants also make them good place for white inhabitants. The result is that most traces of the Osage villages are covered up by more modern construction. An example is the tall brick hospital in Washington, Missouri which sits on the south bank of the Missouri River right where Lewis and Clark said an Osage village used to be. The old village is gone without a trace.

Teresa Maddux did a wonderful job of research for Lebanon High School's *Bittersweet Magazine*. I'm borrowing some of her findings to tell you about Wyota, an Osage village built beside a sacred sinkhole where Lebanon stands now. Teresa tells us about how Wyota was first visited by white men, Franklin Watts, Pierre Marriot, and John Jeffries, in 1795 and their descriptions tell us much.

They wrote that the Osage village was divided into two semicircles with an avenue between them. Thus the entire village was a very large circle. People who live on the north half of the circle were the sky people. Those in the south side were the earth people. Each group had its own chief. In each semicircle there were seven rows of seven lodges. In other words there were 49 families in each community and 98 families in the village. Every door of every lodge faced east to welcome Wah-Kon-Tah, Grandfather the Sun. And these lodges were huge. Called longhouses, a typical lodge was 100 feet long. On hunting trips, the Osage lived in portable wigwams.

Each morning the entire village chanted loud sing-song prayers at dawn. Emotion ran high and even the dogs would howl with the chanting. After the prayers, the women began to work in the garden spaces all around the village. Each family used about ½ acre. The braves showed the white men the "The Hill that Sees Fires." Here a hill sloped upward and a very tall tree grew up from it. Climbing this tree allowed a lookout to see for many miles around. At night the fires of the neighboring village could be seen. It was said to be about 50 miles away.

When a village had more than 98 families, someone had to leave. Usually this would be the newlyweds – the newest families. They would often join with other new families from neighboring villages to start an entirely new community. Some elders would always go to live in the newest villages to serve as chiefs and to guide the younger new families in their quests. I envy Watts, Marriot, and Jeffries and their visit to Wyota.

Sixty Five: Tree Farms

Ceres, the goddess of agriculture stands atop our state capitol building. This is in recognition of the importance of farming in our state. We all know about livestock farming and crop farming but have you ever thought about tree farming? It's big business around here.

Now, we've probably all seen Christmas tree farms. They're very pretty at any time of year and they're usually fairly small because they are so labor-intensive. A Christmas tree farm requires that you trim, prune, and improvise every day. The market has become so competitive that imagination is a major part of any successful operation. Then comes the three or four day rush of cutting and shipping right before Thanksgiving. Your entire year's work boils down to just a few days in November and December.

Tree farming is much different for hardwoods like oak or walnut. For one thing a top quality walnut log sells for thousands of dollars. A good walnut farm will have trees planted on the north slopes of its hills and in little hollows and valleys. Walnuts need a good humus-rich soil and good drainage. To grow tall and straight the trees also need about 20 feet between them and then they need to be thinned out to about forty feet between the trees.

Early on, the crooked, forked, or diseased trees need to be thinned but they don't have much value except for firewood. Later the thinning involves trees which have considerable value and thinning actually becomes a profitable exercise. Mostly it's a waiting game while the trees grow to a valuable size. The longer you wait, the more valuable the tree. However, while you wait, the trees drop nuts which have a value of their own.

Probably the hardest work on a tree farm of any kind is the pruning. It is a skill and it requires a knowledge which is gained only with experience. The pruned material also requires a lot of handling. The higher up on the tree that can be pruned – the more valuable the log.

Animals are the main enemies of the tree farmer. Hawks sit on the tops of young trees and watch for prey. This often breaks off the tops and ruins the sapling. Rabbits also destroy saplings by eating the bark. This is especially true in the late winter when other food is scarce. Grazing animals love to eat the tops off the youngest trees.

Squirrels, on the other hand, can be very helpful as they are constantly planting nuts and starting new trees. To this point though, they haven't been cooperative enough to plant the new ones twenty feet apart and in straight rows as required. There's the next project for you guys and gals in the Department of Natural Resources.

Sixty Six: Gone But Not Forgotten

My wife and I had an old tape in the car stereo the other day and were surprised to hear a song about an out-dated instrument – the percolator. Remember that one? That was followed by one called The Typewriter. Another gone-but-not-forgotten machine. We talked about that fact and then came the next song. It was called The Syncopated Clock. Imagine that, clocks used to go tick tock.

That started me thinking about some things from back when. Most I miss and others I don't. For instance I miss Studebakers, Oldsmobiles, and Plymouths. The Studebaker especially had a very distinct personality. I sometimes think that it was just a little too European for its day. I think the Studebaker Avanti was one of the best ever built.

Something else I miss is frosty window panes. I love our new draft-free multi-paned windows but was anything ever so wondrous as swirling flowery ice crystals across your favorite window on a winter's morning?

Here's one to think about. Do you remember bunkers? I remember them as big old concrete things to be buried in someone's back yard so they could survive atomic blasts. They were creepy to think about. They stirred all sorts of ethical debates. And everyone kind of wanted one. Well, if you haven't noticed, they're coming back. Some folks buy them as a protection against terrorist attacks like dirty bombs or biological weapon releases. Most folks however have acknowledged that those disaster bunkers make wonderful tornado shelters.

Those bunkers and even the old underground storm shelters used to be stocked with lots and lots of home-canned foods. There is something else I miss. Who cans their own food anymore? I know that a few people do. When I go to church socials I recognize the quality and goodness that sometimes shows up in some lady's home-canned contribution. We still can apple butter and I'm hoping that my recently retired wife will can the results of her vegetable gardening efforts.

Porch swings will always be on my list of goodness gone by. Anybody of any age could share a porch swing with anyone else. You couldn't be angry or confrontational while gliding on a shady porch. Day or night, Spring, Summer, or Fall, porch swings brought people together. For that matter, front porches brought people together but we don't see many front porches on the newer houses, do we? A neighbor commented about my mother's new front porch. "Now that's a sittin' porch." he said. How long has it been since sittin' was a worthwhile objective or a positive adjective to be applied to something. We've lost something there.

Aren't there some things that we'll never pine for? I don't think that I'll ever miss those long sticky strings of fly paper. I don't think that any of us will ever look back longingly at outhouses in the heat of summer or in the cold of winter. I remember chasing the mosquito trucks down the street and dancing and playing in the fog which belched out. Of course that was D.D.T. It was fun but I don't long to do it again. I'll never miss scratchy records or changing tires. Aren't you glad that the new ones are so much better?

Here's one that I am going to miss. Incandescent light bulbs. I hate going over to those little twisty, dull, things that are supposed to be better for us. Give me a nice clean bright light anytime. Bottom line – When you start worrying about what all we've given up, drive a car from back in the 50s or 60s. The new ones are better in a million ways. All in all, I would have to say that these changes I brought up today happen as our world becomes a better place.

Sixty Seven: Bringing Yeast to the Frontier

How different it must have been to live on a frontier! When you needed something you would have to create it. There were no stores and sometimes no neighbors to fall back on. Even if there were stores, there were few people with money to spend at the store. People on the frontier were a cashless society.

I don't think that you or I could have survived in a time and place where we had to make everything we needed. Even after you cut the trees and built your shelter, you still had to pull the stumps and plow the land just to get ready to plant a garden. Even if all that went well, how would you keep the wild animals from eating the garden before you could? Even if you could do all those things and had a little grain to show for your efforts, you might find out that you still couldn't bake bread because the nearest yeast was hundreds of miles and weeks away from you.

German settlers knew how to make yeast from hops flowers. There was never a shortage of potato rolls and potato bread in any of those German communities along the Missouri Valley because of the availability of yeast. Hops are a nettle related to hemp and mulberry plants. They grow best in sandy coastal areas so it's a testament to the Germans that they were able to have hops on hand in the middle of the continent like this.

Too much air (in the form of bubbles) can be a problem for rising breads made with yeast so kneading was an important part of preparation for baking. One woman remembers that her mother was especially careful to get rid of bubbles. She named each of her loaves after each of her children and then spanked them all soundly before baking.

Most other Missourians didn't or couldn't have hops with them. They had to bring "everlasting yeast" and keep it alive.

I want to share with you a little story written down by one of my ancestors about how her family, in 1843, brought yeast to the wilderness. Mary Jane (Allen) Mosher said, "In preparing for making bread in the new home, my grandmother said her mother and aunts took freshly boiled dish towels and immersed them in a big batch of 'spook' yeast." This was the soft batter which was always held over from one baking to the next. It is often called sour dough. She said, "The dish towels with batter were hung up in the hot sun until they were thoroughly dried and could be rolled up and packed away for the trip."

In <u>many</u> ways like this, pioneers planned, prepared, worked, and organized so when the journey was over, this new place could become a new home – with fresh baked bread and all. I don't envy them a bit but I admire them a great deal!

Sixty Eight: The Stolen Watermelon

I haven't been one to steal things at many times in my life but this is the story of four small town Missouri boys, including myself, who strayed from the straight and narrow. We were teenagers and driving around town on a summer night and we did what most teenagers do. We complained that there wasn't anything to do. Then one of the boys said that he had never stolen a watermelon. Well, none of us had. We decided to change that.

There was a big problem however. We didn't know where any watermelon patches were. Finally we settled for a pile of watermelons stacked outside the IGA store. The store was closed so we grabbed one and drove off to the ruins of an old farm house. There we sacrificed to the watermelon god by breaking it into four pieces and consuming it. It really wasn't much fun but we did it and went on home.

The next morning I told my parents what I had done. My father asked for details and then reminded me that the two brothers who owned the store were good friends of our family and had always been nice to us. I told him that I knew that and that I was thinking about putting a dollar in the mail to cover the cost of the theft.

Dad would have nothing to do with that! He insisted that I go up to the store and make the payment and the apology in person. Well, I was way to busy for that. I thought up all sorts of reasons why I wouldn't be able to do it in person. A note in the mail would be fine. To my family that was not an acceptable option.

The next day I procrastinated as much as I could but finally made my way to the IGA store and asked to speak with either Lou or Jim. I found one of the brothers sitting in his office going over some figures with an adding machine. He invited me in.

Very nervously I stepped forward and said that I had something that I needed to apologize for. He hardly looked up and asked, "Is this about that watermelon last night?" How did he know? This was before the days of surveillance cameras. Had someone seen us?

I replied that it was about the melon and that I was really sorry. I told him that I came by to pay for it. He explained to me that the apology was appreciated but that I didn't need to pay for it. I told him that I did need to pay for it. Now I was really getting nervous.

He again refused the payment but I knew that when I went home, my parents would specifically ask if I had paid for the stolen melon. I had to pay for it no matter what. I just stepped forward and put the sweaty crumpled dollar on his desk and apologized once more before I left.

Just as I got out the door he called my name. I turned around. "What now?" I wondered. He said, "Thanks for the apology but this is the fourth time this morning that I've been paid for that watermelon." Every child should be so lucky as to be raised by being immersed in small town Midwestern values.

Sixty Nine: Child Rearing, Ozark Style

Here's a challenge for you. Go to any really old church and glance at their records from the 1800s. You will see an amazing number of infant deaths. Also there are far too many deaths for young women where "childbirth" is given as the cause of death. Little kids have always had a hard time getting through infancy but it is not always just because of natural reasons. Our strange beliefs also play a part.

In the Ozarks it was believed that children, if they were to survive, must develop a case of hives while they were infants. Mothers would stay in bed for several days after childbirth and assign the infant care to the oldest daughter, the granny, or whoever else might be available to help. In order to bring on the hives people would give the children special teas made of sheep manure or mouse parts. Of course these remedies were often fatal.

Stomach bands were considered essential for all newborns. It was thought that a baby could never be handled without a stomach band. These cotton bands were worn for protection until the umbilical cord dropped off. Babies were not allowed to cry loudly or for very long because this might cause the naval to protrude. I guess they preferred "insies."

One woman describing various worm medicine teas made of catnip, onions, and Jerusalem oak seeds said, "It would pretty near kill you, let alone the worms. It would really get rid of them."

We've all seen pictures from those days when all of the children wore dresses - Even the boys. That made it easier to change the babies. It also allowed room for a diaper pad which was an old blanket put under the dress to soak up overflows. To avoid tripping, they wore shorter dresses as they began to walk. Many of us from all over the state remember shirts, dresses and clothing made from carefully selected feed bags. Did you get to choose your own feed bag?

Living in a rural home meant that a mother would sometimes have to come up with ways to occupy little children for a few minutes while she tended to other things. One way was to make a little pacifier called a sugar tit. Another way was to give the child a feather with molasses on it. It would stick to one hand and then the other for long periods of time.

I remember well my grandmother's way of keeping me and my cousins busy. First was to let us go outside and be kids. If we ever got a little too wild . . . When we got a little too wild, she would call us in and sit us around the big dinner table. Then out would come the jars of buttons. We never knew why Grandma needed all those buttons strung on long strings and arranged by size or color. We never thought to ask. We just respected her so much that when she needed help with her button stringing chores, we did everything we could to help. After a few minutes of stringing, a reminder to behave, and maybe a little snack, we were back outside and playing. Child rearin' Ozark style was sometimes a wonderful thing!

Seventy: Making Do

"Use it up. Wear it out. Make it do or do without." Did your grandmother ever say anything like that? It sounds like something either one of my grandmothers could have said. "Use it up. Wear it out. Make it do or do without." That generation, the one that made it through the Great Depression and World War II, and the ones who grew up during that time look at things differently than the rest of us. I'm afraid that we are entirely too fond of throwing things away and replacing them.

My mother tells of how she and each of her four sisters would take turns wearing the same coat but it would be made over each year. One might have thought that those Wood girls each got a new coat every year. Actually they were just good at making do.

My father and his siblings used to walk through the woods to school each day. When they got to the road, they would sit down and put on their shoes. They would save pride by being seen in shoes but wouldn't waste precious shoe leather in the woods. They could make a pair of shoes last longer than you or me.

If you would take a moment, you could remember some way that the older generations were far more frugal than we are. Your parents and grandparents don't understand why it's OK for us to be so wasteful. They don't understand why it's important for us to have closets with too many clothes and four bedrooms for two people. They just don't understand why each family member needs his or her own telephone, television, and computer.

Many older people don't believe us when we say it's better to replace socks than darn them. They don't believe us when we say that leftover food is not worth using. They don't believe that turning the heat up so we can wear summer clothing in the winter is the smart way to do things. We really need to get specific and explain to them why we have things figured out and they don't.

One thing that older people do understand is this. They know the difference between fashion and fad. They know that stylish things of all kinds hold their classic good looks, their worth, and their value. They know that what passes for style is often just a fad and too temporary to even have value. Even classic sayings can have lasting worth. Such as, "Use it up. Wear it out. Make it do or do without." That's one that could change your life – and make it better.

One of my favorite people was an old codger named Montie Potts. To him, frugality was a game – and he was good at it. During his life Montie accumulated a good deal of wealth but people who didn't know him well would never guess. Sometimes he would begin a statement with, "Now I'm just a poor man but . . ." A little smile across his face would belie the fact that he was anything but poor. That was his little secret and he reveled in it. I think there's a lesson there for all of us. If done in moderation, saving and making do combined with a good dose of humility can put little smiles across <u>our</u> faces too.

Seventy One: Susan Elizabeth Blow

You may have heard of Susan Elizabeth Blow. There are lots of streets named Blow and many schools named Blow in her honor. It's just that her accomplishments were years ago and her achievements have become such a normal part of American life that we forget that it was her who brought something to us.

Susan was a lucky girl! She grew up in one of the richest families in the city during St. Louis' Gilded Age. She also got to travel – even to Europe. While in Germany she saw a new idea in action. They had what they called gardens for the little children to grow in. Little classrooms where the emphasis was not academic things but in the pre-academic things like developing the social and physical skills which would make school success more likely. These programs were called child gardens and the German way of saying that is Kindergarten.

Miss Blow had always been interested in education so she visited several kindergartens to check them out as much as possible. Then she brought the idea back to Missouri. The superintendent of schools, William Harris encouraged her and allowed her to open a kindergarten at the Des Peres School in St. Louis. Susan taught without pay so she could hire a paid helper and soon two un-paid helpers joined the effort.

Kindergarten made such a difference in the children's achievement that the St. Louis Public Schools soon had thirty kindergartens operating around the city and there was demand for more. This actually created a problem.

Susan Blow was aware that teaching kindergarten was not like teaching in other grades. The curriculum, teaching style, and teaching techniques all had to be different. This required teacher training on a large scale. Again Susan went to Mr. Harris and asked if she could start a teacher-training institution for St. Louis.

She opened this new facility to train kindergarten teachers but other levels of instruction were soon added and teachers were being trained for all grade levels. This institution is known today as the Harris State College. St. Louis was now the only city in the U.S. to have free kindergartens available in the public schools and Harris College was training kindergarten teachers for work across the country.

Another Missouri educator, Phoebe Apperson Hearst, from nearby Franklin County picked up on Susan's work and advocated for more kindergartens in America. Mrs. Hearst had started a group called the National Congress of Mothers and this turned into the National P.T.A. Through the P.T.A. Phoebe spurred the growth of kindergartens across America. She amplified the work of Susan Blow.

In a very short time it had become much easier for children across America to begin their school experience smoothly and successfully, thanks to the pioneering and tireless work of Susan Elizabeth Blow.

Seventy Two: The Fire of 1849

After the San Francisco earthquake in 1906 a great fire destroyed much of the city. In Chicago a great fire destroyed much of that city in 1871. Mrs. O'Leary took a bum rap on that one. It's been proven that her cow had nothing to do with it. There have been great fires in American cities and others like London and Tokyo. However, one of the biggest was in Missouri and we seem to have forgotten all about it.

In 1849 the St. Louis riverfront was a bustling place packed with steamboats lined up in close order all along the levee. At times more than 150 boats could be tied up at the St. Louis levee. The tonnage going through that port was second only to New York. This particular year saw two unusual situations in addition to the population and business boom. A flood of '49ers was funneling through and arranging for transportation west to the gold fields. There was also a cholera epidemic now well underway.

Then at 9:00 AM on May 17, 1849. Disaster struck. The steamboat White Cloud caught fire. The fire began to spread from one boat to another because they were crowded so closely together. Then the mooring ropes on the White Cloud burned through and she began to drift downstream bumping into and setting one boat on fire after another.

The fire began to spread through the wooden buildings along the riverfront and then the entire east side of the city. For the first time in Missouri's history a "firestorm" was created. The heated air rose and pulled in air from around it. With the blaze creating its own wind there seemed little if any way to stop it. To make it worse, the firemen were suffering from extreme exhaustion.

Desperate situations call for desperate measures. The fire department created a plan. They would blow up a number of buildings in the path of the fire and create a firebreak. With this zone in place the fire might not be able to jump over and ignite other buildings.

They began packing stores, businesses, and warehouses with kegs of black powder and blowing up the buildings. Captain Thomas Targee of Fire Company 5 was not one to send his men into places or situations that he wouldn't go himself so he was setting off the charges. While he was spreading powder in the Phillips Music Store, the last one to be blown up, it exploded prematurely and killed the Fire Captain.

The result of all the destruction was in some ways positive. The French part of the city with narrow winding streets and wooden buildings was completely gone. With them out of the way, a new water and sewage system were installed. It was ordered that all future buildings be constructed of brick or stone. Today's system of wide squared streets was begun and St. Louis was finally a truly American city.

Seventy Three: Festivals Back Then

Imagine living on the frontier and what your days would be like. For one thing, you would work from dawn to dark. For another you would do this almost every day. Your neighbors might be miles away. Even if they were closer, with no good roads and forests full of dangers, you didn't go to visit very often. How you would look forward to special days!

Camp meetings must have been wonderful! For one thing they lasted for several days. You had to bring a tent and live in it during the meeting – that's why they were called camp meetings. At these meetings you could hear real preaching and oratory. You could also hear and participate in singing the favorite old-timey hymns and maybe shape note singing. You could enjoy food from campfires and Dutch ovens. You could visit with everyone and the kids could play with hundreds of new friends. Young men and women had an opportunity to meet others that they might never have known.

Brush arbor meetings seem to be the idea of Presbyterian minister, James McGready. He came up with a way to bring religion to people on the frontier. They were usually conducted by a "circuit riding" preacher who traveled through the area serving several small groups of Christians in areas that didn't have a large enough population to support a church.

For these meetings an arbor had to be constructed. This was done by either bending trees over so the tops met each other and then fastening them or by just cutting trees and building a framework of logs. Then the branches, underbrush, or anything else would be thrown on top and a long structure would be prepared. This might be an open pavilion-type structure or a more enclosed leafy tunnel depending on the weather conditions. Either way the attendees would have shelter from the sun, the dew, or even a light rain.

After the horses were un-hitched, watered, and put out to graze, the families would erect the tent or shelter needed for each night. Since these meetings were always done near a fresh water supply, the men might try to catch a few fish while the women prepared supper. The children, of course, made new friends and played all sorts of games.

The preaching was loud and riveting. The singing was hymns which most people knew "by heart." It went on for days or even as long as two weeks as the fervor built. Finally, on the last day, many people followed the preacher down to the stream for Baptism.

Once towns were populated, festivals and celebrations came for many reasons. The 4th of July was big in every community. Local townspeople seemed to look for reasons to get together, be happy, and bond as a community. Celebrations formed a glue which held the communities together.

Seventy Four: The School Marms' Uprising

Dizzy Dean was the most colorful of all of those old Cardinals called "The Gashouse Gang." He truly was a great pitcher and accomplished wonderful things for his club and the fans. He did have a problem however with his ego. Maybe he was covering up for his insecurity or, more likely, he really thought he was the center of the baseball world. Dean actually said, "Anybody who's ever had the privilege of seeing me play knows that I am the greatest pitcher in the world." He could be a little hard to be around.

But he was good. How many pitchers now get 30 wins in a season? Dean did but that was over 70 years ago and no one has done it since. He once got his pay cut for winning only 28! He was heard to ask a batter, "Son, what kind of pitch would you like to miss?" Then he'd wind up his old "soup bone" as he called his arm, and blow the batters away.

He finished his career with the St. Louis Browns and then took an announcing job with CBS radio and television. People loved him. His colorful descriptions of the action were just as much fun as his playing. People would sometimes get their best laughs of the week as they followed their favorite teams.

Dizzy sometimes got into trouble with reporters. He would give them each a different set of facts about an event so they would each have a different story to write. When accused of telling lies to the reporters he replied, Them ain't lies, them's scoops."

Dizzy occasionally got into trouble with sponsors. He once reported, "Sure I eat what I advertise. Sure I eat Wheaties for breakfast. A good bowl of Wheaties with bourbon can't be beat." The main problem he had, however, was with the nation's English teachers.

To Dizzy, the past tense of "slide" was "slud" as in, "He slud into second." He claimed to be speaking, "plain ol' ordinary pinto bean English." Dean described players who throwed balls, and walked to the plate "confidentiality." They looked "hitterish" and "swang" at pitches. After a fowl ball Diz had runners returning to their "respectable" bases.

At first he was defiant toward the teachers. When they challenged him on his constant use of the word "ain't" he said, "Let the teachers teach English and I will teach baseball. There's a lot of people in the United States who say 'isn't' and they ain't eating. Another time he said, "I ain't never met anybody that didn't know what ain't means."

In the end, the massive walking ego had to eat a huge portion of humble pie and it seemed to make him a better person. The battle with the school marms, as he called them, was the hardest of his career. But he came to terms with his own limitations and America loved him all the more.

Seventy Five: Missouri Sports Stumpers

I know that many people who are interested in this kind of subject matter are not too interested in sports trivia. However, some of this is so unusual that I'll bet you like it after all.

For instance, there was once a young man who went to high school in Missouri and was such a standout that he was picked as a High School All-American. Then he went on to college. Again he played here in Missouri and was named a College All-American. After graduation he decided to play professional basketball and he played his pro ball here in Missouri. And, what do you know, he was named an All-Pro. Can you name this exceptional athlete? Can you name the championship teams for which he played? Here's a big hint. All three teams were in St. Louis.

If you said Easy Ed McCauley, you were correct. He played on championship teams for the St. Louis University High School Jr. Bills, St. Louis University Billikens, and the St. Louis Hawks. By the way, after retirement, he became the youngest man ever inducted into the Hall of Fame.

There were some World Series games which were played between Missouri teams. Can you name any of those times? The I-70 series was a fairly recent one in which the Royals beat the Cardinals 4 games to 3. Way back in the 40s it happened again but it wasn't those two teams. Can you think of who it was?

If you said St. Louis vs. St. Louis, you are right. The Cardinals beat the Browns in 1944 but where did they play the games? OK the Cardinals played in Sportsman's Park alright but when they played in the Browns' home park, where was that? Correct. Sporstman's Park was the home field for both teams.

Then there's Eddie Gaedel who was one of the most memorable athletes on the Browns. Can you remember what was so special about Eddie? Can you remember his historic uniform number?

If you said he was number 1/8, you're good. He was a "ringer" brought in to stand at the plate and get walked. Prior to the game, the owner brought a giant birthday cake out to the middle of the field and said he had a new "Brownie" for the manager. Out popped three foot, seven inch Eddie Gaedel. Eddie's strike zone was so small that he was walked in the first inning and then was taken out for a pinch runner. That ended the career of number 1/8 but the "ex-big leaguer" made thousands of dollars with talk shows and endorsements after that.

Here's one last stumper. Can you think of the only person who played for both the St. Louis Cardinals professional football team and the St. Louis Cardinals baseball team? OK, I'll give you a gigantic hint. He also played for the St. Louis Blues. If you're really good you'll be able to tell what he played for each team.

If you're not from the St. Louis area this really isn't fair, I know. The player is Ernie Hayes. Does that sound familiar? It will when I tell you what he played. For all three teams he played . . . the Wurlitzer. He was the organist for decades with each team.

Seventy Six: Amazing Hatcheries

One of my favorite memories as a boy was visiting at the Cackle Hatchery. The great shelves of eggs and chicks in various stages of development were always a joy. There weren't just chickens of course. They also hatched turkeys, quail, guineas, ducks, and lots of special varieties. Incubators were big sellers for home use at one time but the hatcheries got so good at boxing chicks for shipment by mail, that many people began ordering live chicks rather hatching them themselves.

In the past every farm family had chickens and even in the cities and towns, people would often have a coop in the back yard. Now of course chickens are found mostly on farms. Chicks are so vulnerable to predators that farmers purchased them in large numbers. Hawks, pigs, foxes, wild dogs, coyotes and other predators reduced the numbers of chicks and some would die from parasites or exposure. Therefore, if a farmer wanted to end up with 100 fryers or broilers, he might order 500 chicks from a hatchery.

In the recent past there were hatcheries spread across the country and states like Missouri had many hatcheries doing business on a fairly local basis. Now there are just over 300 hatcheries in the nation. That's an average of about 6 per state. Missouri still has thirteen. The hatcheries now are usually very large operations and those 300 produce over nine billion (with a b) broiler chicks each year. That's about 30 million broilers for the average hatchery. Why so many? Because we each eat over 76 pounds of chicken a year!

We also have to remember that, in addition to those numbers, we are also turning out about 421 million egg-producing chicks each year and about 45 million turkeys each year.

In spite of great demand, there were no hatcheries west of the Mississippi. Then Clinton, Missouri became known as the "Baby Chick Capital of the World." This was due to the success of the Booth Hatchery and two competitors. The booth hatchery started in 1913 as the project of a high school student to earn a little spending money. The booth facility eventually had an incubator which could hold a million eggs at a time. At one time three different railroads were serving the Booth Hatchery with specially built flat cars for hauling crates of live chicks.

The founder, Royal Booth, constantly worked to improve his operation and, through selective breeding, soon took an industry-leading average of 150 eggs per year to a much higher level. His new breeds could lay as many as 248 eggs per year. Since Chickens are such a great source of eggs and meat, the business continued to flourish even through the depression and hundreds of people had good jobs during the toughest of times. In the 1950s Clinton's hatcheries were shipping 110 million chicks a year. Then conditions changed. Supermarkets, meat processing, and graded eggs spelled the end for many hatcheries.

The largest hatcheries now have only about five employees each. What a change from days gone by!

Seventy Seven: Springs Have Sprung

One of the greatest things about Missouri is the number of beautiful springs across the state. Some come gushing out of flatland like the artesian well in Columbia. Others flow from beautiful little valleys in the Ozarks. Either way they are wonders of nature but I'm not sure we all appreciate just how wonderful they are.

One of the most surprising things is where the water comes from for the springs. I remember as a child playing in a big riverbed called Goodwin Hollow. The funny thing is that it never seemed to have any water. It turns out that Goodwin Hollow is something called a "losing stream." These are fairly common in the Ozarks and they will drain a large watershed but the water seeps into the ground faster than it can travel downstream. It just loses itself into the riverbed and disappears. Goodwin Hollow actually provides underground water for nearby Bennett Spring and distant Ha Ha Tonka Spring.

Another amazing thing is the size of some of the springs. Meramec Spring gushes 100 million gallons of water a day. This spring was discovered very early in the state's history. An ironmonger met Indians decorated with an iron-based paint. They told him where they got their iron (hematite) and by 1826 the first iron furnace west of the Mississippi was operating by the stream.

I spent much of my boyhood along the stream at Bennett Spring. This beauty pumps 103 million gallons of cold clear water into the little valley each day. The hole from which the water flows is 80 feet deep and goes horizontally for 130 feet underground. From there no one has been able to explore. The water flows with such strength and swirls so much flint that divers can proceed no further.

Greer Spring is a little-known treasure. It pours out 222 million gallons a day from two holes which are about 300 feet apart. Greer produces a stream which drops rapidly downhill at such a pace that boating cannot be allowed. Two deaths have occurred from people trying to take boats onto that water. At one time there was a mill at the spring and the trail to it was so steep that specially trained oxen were employed to carry grain and flour up and down the trail without people driving them.

The big daddy of Missouri's springs is appropriately named Big Spring. At 286 million gallons a day, it's a natural wonder. In 1803 Pocahontas Randolph went looking for the spring. He had been told by the Indians about "a spring that roared." He didn't find it. It remained just a mysterious rumor until 1913 when Henry Sawyer bought a rough possibly worthless piece of back-country land and discovered the spring that roared. It is now owned and managed by the National Park Service.

Many of these places are publicly owned and ready to meet your needs as you picnic, camp, or just spend a day. You really should plan to see them.

Seventy Eight: Jim the Wonder Dog

They say that the average dog can understand about 100 words. We've all seen things that certain dogs can do that are impressive but the most impressive dog ever was known as Jim the Wonder Dog.

Jim lived in Marshall, Missouri back in 1925. He was more than just a really smart animal. We've all seen those but Jim was something special. Listen to some of the feats that Jim could routinely perform.

When hunting he knew which fields had birds in them and which ones did not. Samuel Van Arsdale, Jim's owner, just let Jim choose the fields for hunting and he said he was never disappointed.

You probably know that dogs are color blind. They can only see black and white and shades of gray. But Jim was different. You could put objects in any order and change the order but Jim could always pick out whatever color you asked him for.

Jim could also find people's cars for them. All you had to do was to tell him the license plate number and he'd go right to it. You could tell him the make of the car and it's color and he'd find it for you. You could even point out the owner of the car and he would find the correct car. He may have been doing that one by scent.

If you would ask him to find a particular kind of tree or shrub, he would find one for you. He could even locate a business for you if you would tell him the name.

Since dogs can't speak, answers would often have to be written on papers for him. He could always choose the paper with the correct answer. In case you think his owner was tipping him off, the answers were sometimes written in languages Mr. Van Arsdale didn't understand. Jim correctly responded to answers written in English, Italian, French, German, Greek, and Spanish.

In 1936 they decided to see if Jim could pick the winner in the presidential election. Of course he did. They also asked him to indicate who would win the World Series and he did that correctly too.

He was so good at predicting, the people decided to see if he could predict the winner for the Kentucky Derby. He did. He also did the next year and the next. They asked him to choose the winner for seven years and he was correct all seven times. As if there were no limits to his abilities, he could routinely indicate correctly the sex of a baby before it was born.

Jim was examined by scientists and veterinarians at the University of Missouri in Columbia. Except for the fact that he responded to their commands given in five different languages, he seemed normal in every way. Hardly!

Seventy Nine: The St. Louis Massacre

It's one of the truths of history that the victor gets to write the history books. Maybe that's why so few people have heard of the St. Louis Massacre. In a very short form, here's what happened that day on May 10, 1861.

Missouri's Legislature had declared its intention to remain neutral during the War Between the States. Looking back, that would have been a wonderful thing for the state which was destined to see 1,106 battles and skirmishes on her soil. However, this situation was one which aroused strong emotions on both sides. Radical people were to make choices which dragged the rest of the population kicking and screaming into the fray.

Southern sympathizers in St. Louis felt that they were being ignored and their ideas not given recognition by the northern officers who were controlling the city from their headquarters at Jefferson Barracks. In order to show their feelings and to demonstrate their sheer numbers, the southerners staged a march from the city out to an open area where St. Louis University now stands. There they camped overnight and practiced marching and forming into units. It was a demonstration of strength but, truth be told, their numbers were very small compared to the number of Union troops in the area.

Captain Nathaniel Lyon heard a rumor that the men at the camp were planning to seize the weapons being held at the St. Louis Armory so he decided to investigate. To do this he dressed up as an old woman, hid his bushy beard behind a veil, and skulked around the campgrounds for much of the night. The next morning, the hotheaded Lyon decided to march his troops out to confront the men at the camp. He surrounded the 800 men with 10,000 regulars and volunteers, and demanded that they surrender. The southern sympathizers were not prepared for any conflict and they were greatly outnumbered so they immediately surrendered. Then Lyon made the decision to humiliate his captives.

He marched them back into St. Louis between two columns of his own men as a demonstration of his power and their weakness. A crowd gathered along the route of the procession and they, hating to see the men treated so badly, began to shout insults at the mostly German Union troops. Then the crowd grew more boisterous and began spitting at the soldiers. A large group of citizens followed the procession and in this crowd were people from both sides. William Tecumseh Sherman was there. You will remember him as the northern General who led "Sherman's March to the Sea." Ulysses S. Grant, who became the commander of all northern armies and President of the United States, was also part of the crowd.

Then a shot rang out. It was a pistol shot but no one knows who fired it. That's when Captain Lyon ordered his men to fire into the crowd. Sherman threw his son to the ground and jumped on top of him to keep him from being shot. Ninety civilians were shot that day and twenty-eight of them died from their wounds. The next day Union troops were sent out again to keep the peace and seven more citizens were shot. News of the slaughter went out by telegraph to courthouses across the state and huge numbers of enlistments for the Southern cause took place on those two days.

On the 12th, a peace conference was called and Lyon said that rather than accept the limited role of the army in a neutral state, he would see, "every man, woman and child in the state dead and buried." The whole idea of Missouri remaining neutral was over.

Eighty: Town & County Stumpers

A while back I tried to stump you on some Missouri sports trivia. Let's change the subject and try some different ones. For instance, Missouri has 114 counties. Why are there so many counties? The answer is that when they established our present counties they wanted every resident to be within a short horseback ride to the county seat so that they could go roundtrip in one day.

Which of the 114 counties is physically the largest? Well, Texans always like to brag about being big and in Missouri, Texas County is our biggest. Do you remember it's county seat? It's Houston. Of all our counties, do you know which one is the smallest? The smallest by far is

Worth County on the Iowa border. With only 2000 residents, it's small in population too.

There is one city which is in no county at all. Do you remember which city that is? You're right – St. Louis city is its own county. It is completely separate from St. Louis County which surrounds it.

Some railroad workers hid a barrel of Bourbon whiskey in a place along the tracks. After the railroad was built, a town grew up right there where the treasure was hidden. Do you know which town got it's name from that popular barrel? That was easy . . . Bourbon, Missouri.

A salt lick was a great place for deer hunting and later a great place for grazing livestock. One such place had a town grow up next to a salt lick. The town's name was The Lick. What is it's present day name? If you said Licking, Missouri, you are right. Boone's Lick, Saline and other places got their names in similar ways.

People in Laclede County wanted to name a new town and there was a lot of competition as everyone had their own ideas about a suitable name. The result was that an appropriate name was selected – Competition. Just the opposite was true when Franklin County decided to build a new town in the middle of the county to serve as a county seat. There was a lot of competition for the name but it all ended in a feeling of unity or union. So, the county seat is Union, Missouri.

When the Union Pacific Railroad came through the area they wanted to start a new town just west of Eureka. They thought about naming the place Union in honor of the railroad but there already was a Union, Missouri in that very county so they named the new place . . . You guessed it, Pacific, Missouri.

Another argument took place when the folks of Lakeville, Missouri realized that the town would never grow being as far from the railroad as they were. They considered themselves the kind of advanced thinkers who could be flexible and pragmatic. They suggested that the town move to the tracks. Not everyone agreed. The result is that the advanced thinkers group moved and formed a new town by the tracks and named it Advance, Missouri. The stay-behind folks then named their town Toga. We know which one lasted through time don't we.

Eighty One: Looking the Other Way

A boy stood in front of the congregation at the little country church. He was as nervous as a porcupine in a balloon factory. It was his first time to be the lay liturgist. Sure enough he made some mistakes and got a little flustered but everyone appreciated what he did. My wife commented, "Isn't it nice to have a little place like this for people to break in? A place where we can look the other way when someone makes little mistakes?

Small churches and small towns are like that. They are forgiving and even protective of their own. I was told about a little church which had one claim to fame. It's organist had more consecutive years in her position than any other organist in the state. The young minister who told this story substituted in that church one Sunday and had his service carefully planned and the bulletin was carefully checked before printing. When everyone stood to sing the first hymn, they waited to see what the organist was going to play and then they all hurried to find that hymn and join in. It didn't matter what the minister wanted. The organist played what she felt like. Everyone just accepted that. Idiosyncrasies are overlooked in small churches.

At a gathering in another small town I got out of my car and locked it before going into the church for the meeting. The local minister reminded me to leave my car unlocked with the keys in the ignition. He explained that large farm machinery often comes through the little streets and the farmer might need to move my car out of the way. He'd park it real close by.

In my hometown there was a man with coke-bottle glasses who used to stand in the busiest intersections directing traffic. I tried to figure out his method and finally asked him how he knew which cars to send and when. He explained that he just watched those colored lights. "Red means that it's time for the cars to go and green means that it's time for the walking people to go. Red is for cars and green is for people." Sure he was dangerous but night after night he was out there and the locals would just smile and wait for his help.

In another Missouri town people at one church learned to lock their cars while they were in the church. An elderly neighbor lady used to come out and go through the cars and take things which interested her. Afterwards her husband would collect the articles and bring them back to the owners. Sure the lady had a problem. But it was the community's problem. In no time at all the lady's family and the church-goers had made little adjustments in how they did things and the problem was no more. In small towns we can often solve the problem with a little compassion and an ability to look the other way.

Now I'm all for people who do wrong or those who refuse to do things in safe and approved ways having to face the consequences. But, isn't it really nice if we can be accepting and understanding and have the small town's ability to just look the other way?

Eighty Two: Show Me the Money

Records show that when some of my ancestors got engaged the groom-to-be went to the courthouse and posted "forty pounds current money" to demonstrate his serious intent to marry. I used to wonder, "Why forty pounds?" Why not dollars? Pounds have never been American currency.

The truth is that the use of money in America used to be kind of a fluid thing. Many people didn't use money at all – especially on the frontier. It was often a cashless society. You could trade goods for your services. An example would be a doctor getting paid for his house call with a chicken. You could trade your goods for other goods. An example would be a trading post where you could turn in pelts and exchange them for a set of knives. Or you could actually use cash. The kind of cash didn't seem to matter much.

The American dollar has not always been secure and valuable. In times past people could easily purchase things with English or Spanish coins. Historian, Stanley Wilke, has found records in an old store in Franklin County showing charges to customers in dollars, bits, and picayunes. The dollar we know about. A bit was half of a quarter or 12 ½ cents. A picayune was a Spanish coin which was worth about five cents. This Franklin County merchant was allowing ½ of one bit for a picayune. In other words, the picayune was traded for 6 ¼ cents.

Dollars in the old days were huge. So were coins like the penny. In 1927 the dollars became the size we see now. If you would like to see what the old money was like, cut a piece of paper to 3 and 1/16 inches by 7 and 3/8 inches long. Copper pennies were as big as silver dollars. Did you know that some of our "coins" were made of paper? In the Civil War there was small paper currency in denominations like 10 cents and 50 cents.

Now, some of us still remember and still have some coins which are made of plastic or cardboard. These mills were issued mostly by states and were used for paying taxes. They didn't just round things up to the nearest penny. You were expected to produce some mills for your sales tax or give them a penny and get change.

Counterfeiting has always been a problem. When various banks in various cities produced their own U.S. currency this was especially so. Imagine getting a dollar printed by a bank in Omaha and another printed by a mercantile company in Santa Fe. If they looked a little different it might not be too surprising. Now of course all U.S. currency is printed by the Bureau of Printing and Engraving and it should look just the same.

Now, counterfeiters will always try to copy money but it's becoming harder and harder. They also want to copy fairly common bills and bills which are large enough to make it worth their while. Twenties and hundreds work well. But, did you know that one Missourian, A.B. Small, was, after his death, discovered to have spent his life minting counterfeit coins in his little backwoods shack? You have to wonder – why bother?

Eighty Three: Pigs as Lard Producers

Some of my rural family members will jump me about this one. I plan to tell you a few things about pigs and they'll say, "Any fool knows that stuff." I'm betting that I give you some new things to think about.

For one thing, pigs have not always looked the way they do now. Sixty or seventy years ago the really good ones looked a lot like barrels on legs. They were incredibly fat because the fat had value. Sure the hams, pork chops, bacon, and sausage were always good stuff. But the rendered fat, also known as lard, was canned and sold, and used in every part of cooking and used sometimes for lubrication.

High in cholesterol and calories, lard has been replaced by various vegetable cooking oils. Some young people say that they would never use lard and don't understand why anyone ever wood. Those people have probably never knowingly tasted the results of cooking with lard. When they have tasted such products, they probably just didn't realize why they tasted so good.

Again, because of the value of lard, the pigs were big round barrels of meat and fat. On a champion hog the fat would hang right down over the face. One old timer was asked how you could tell which end was which. He said, "You just smack it with a stick and see which end squeals."

Lard has some interesting qualities. It lasts for a surprisingly long time. The man who lives where my wife's great-grandparents lived said that he found an old stone jar and thought she might like to have it. She loves stoneware and the fact that it had belonged to her grandmother or great-grandmother made it even more special. A black substance nearly filled the jar but we knew we could scoop it out. After scooping off about an inch of the stuff, a beautiful white smooth cream appeared. It was pure white lard – still good after many decades.

One day I was trying to cook an American-style meal for some folks from South America. I had pork chops, corn-on-the-cob, baked beans, and apple pie with ice cream. They really liked our sweet corn and pie but were disappointed in our pork. I know they were right. When I was there the pork was juicier and tastier. Theirs was delicious while we have bred ours to be dry, healthful, and bland.

Do you remember when ribs were considered to be junk. You ate things like ribs, bologna, and ground beef when you were short on money. That's as silly as when the Pilgrims wouldn't eat lobster. We were really missing some good stuff, weren't we?

I guess we'd have to say that whatever the consumer has asked for, the pork producers have been quick to give us. I'm glad we can have pork without all the fat and cholesterol but we should also realize that our ancestors sometimes experienced some good things that we probably never will.

Eighty Four: Missouri's Champeen Fighter

This must be true because it was told to Bittersweet Magazine by folklorist, Doug Mahnkey. Mr. Mahnkey, like most Ozarkers, would never tell a lie. But he does have a variety of ways to tell the truth. I have shortened this to make it fit.

It seems that a big strappin' young man named Tom down in Stone County just loved to fight. It was more rasslin' than fightin' but he could always came out on top. After he whipped everybody around he declared himself to be the "Champeen Fighter of Missouri."

Then one day he heard of a man just across the line who was supposed to be the Champeen Fighter of Arkansas. Tom saddled up his mule and told his wife, "I plan to challenge this man at Alpena Pass. I'll whip him of course. Then I'll be the champeen of both Missouri and Arkansas. I'll be back in a few days." Then he headed due south for Arkansas.

After asking about, he was pointed in the direction of the right man. When he came to this particular cabin, he asked the wife of the house, "Is this the home of the Champeen Fighter of Arkansas?"

She said that it was but he wasn't there. She said, "He's working in the field just down that hollow. You can go on down. You'll hear him a-carryin' on before you get there. Just follow the sound of his voice and you'll find him a-sowin' oats."

When Tom arrived at the field he rode his mule right up to the rail fence to get a good look at his opponent. He watched as the largest man he had ever seen held a giant bed tick over his shoulder. It was full of seeds and must have weighed a few hundred pounds. It had a small hole in the bottom and as he swayed back and forth, the seeds would scatter across the field. He had a harrow attached to his right ankle and was pulling it behind with every step. He had another big harrow attached to his left ankle. As he walked the harrows would drag through the plowed dirt and cover the seeds.

Swaying and stepping, he was sowing and covering, planting an entire field by himself. He was doing the work of two men and a team of horses. Tom was very impressed! When the Arkansawer got to the fence near Tom, he stopped.

Tom said, "Good morning, sir. I hear you claim to be the Champeen Fighter of Arkansas."

"You heard rightly." The man replied.

Tom said with great ceremony, "Well, Mr. Arkansas Champeen, I rode all the way here today to tell you that you are the Champeen Fighter of Missouri also."

Eighty Five: Nothin' Good About Alf Bolin

An old timer when asked about Alf Bolin said, "There weren't nothin' good about Alf Bolin." It seems true that this character from south Missouri was about as low as they come. He was a snake in the rocks around Forsyth, Missouri.

Not much is known about Bolin when he was young. Something must have happened to his parents because he and his sister were raised by the Bilyeu family near Spokane, Missouri. When the Civil War began, he organized a gang which terrorized the area. Some say that he had about twenty men riding with him. Others say fifty.

If asked, he would say that he was fighting for the Confederacy. It's probably closer to the truth to say that he was fighting against authority. He was just taking advantage of the fact that most of the able-bodied men were away from home and at the war.

At what came to be called Bolin's Rocks or Murder Rocks, the gang ambushed people passing on the road below. He let nothing stop him. No one knows how many he killed during his time along Fox Creek but at least fourteen murders of old men, children, and women have been documented. He also killed at least two soldiers.

Finally the Union Army figured out a way to stop him. A soldier named Zach Thomas went to the home of the Foster family. Mr. Foster was a southern sympathizer and was a prisoner of war. Foster was promised a release if his family would help with the plan to get Alf Bolin. The union soldier, Thomas, was disguised as a Confederate soldier. Thomas pretended to be sick as he stayed for several days hoping that Alf Bolin would appear.

Finally Bolin did come to the house and was hacked with a plowshare by the soldier. They took the body into another room only to discover that he was not dead. So they killed him again. Bolin's life ended at age 21.

When they took the body to Forsyth a street celebration began. The good citizens decapitated Bolin and put the head on a pole in the center of Ozark, Missouri. This was on May 15, 1863. Since that time, people wanting to get married or looking for a good day to celebrate can choose to do so on what has been called Alf Bolin Day. May 15 is a charmed and lucky day in the Forsyth area!

There is one last part of this story. Since the gang was so active and pulled so many robberies, there is a story of loot hidden and marked with the skull of a horse. But only Bolin knew just where to look. Now treasure hunters continue to scour the area along Route JJ, ten miles south of Forsyth.

Any person who finds that treasure will consider it a good thing. But, truth be told, there weren't nothin' good about Alf Bolin.

Eighty Six: Charivari (Shivaree)

As far as I can tell, charivari is a custom which has recently been practiced all over the state and now may have disappeared completely. In Missouri it seems to have been mostly a small town and rural custom. Many of us have participated in or at least seen Charivaris. Now they're a very distant memory. I wonder why.

The charivaris I witnessed were just a lot of friends celebrating with the newlyweds. The groom would give his bride a ride down the street in a wheelbarrow. Everyone else would be singing, shouting, honking horns and making noise. Creativity and originality in noisemaking was sought after. Stanley Wilke tells that one man carried a suckling pig and squeezed its ear and then would loudly squeal in duet with the pig. I was told that the climax used to mean a dunking in a pond. It was probably embarrassing for the newlyweds but just a lot of fun. In Missouri the charivari was sometimes a "welcome home" party after the honeymoon. The origins of the practice are fairly strange.

Originally in France, it was just a celebration. It evolved into a social protest against unacceptable marriages. For instance, the marriage of a widow who didn't mourn long enough, or, a very old man who could not consummate his marriage marrying a very young woman. A young man marrying a wealthy widow beyond childbearing could also spark a charivari.

A very similar custom known as "Riding the 'Stang" was performed for a wife who scolded or beat men. Riding the 'Stang meant that the woman would be forced to sit backward on a horse and then paraded through the streets of town while people mocked her and created noise to call attention to the proceeding.

The origin of the word charivari probably comes from the Romans and it basically means "headache." A similar word in Greek meant head or heavy. These definitions would fit well with the loud noise and boisterous commotion which was a part of every charivari.

So, why did such a widespread custom die out? I have a few ideas. First I think that the amount of money spent on weddings now is prohibitive. With dresses costing hundreds of dollars and even rented clothing for the men, wheelbarrow riding and dunking just may not be an option.

Another reason may be that now the bride and groom have a more formal reception and the wedding party is too busy at the reception hall to go parading down the main street. Also, the bride and groom now are often whisked away to a honeymoon trip. Most people could not afford such things in the past. Maybe we are just too sophisticated. I don't really know anyone who would enjoy a charivari now. They did years ago but I don't think people would now.

One last thought. Maybe we still do a little bit of Charivari. Spraying the couple with rice or bird seed gets more than a little enthusiastic sometimes. Painting the car and tying cans and noisy objects to the car might be all that's left of the thousand-year-old custom – charivari.

Eighty Seven: Buzzards

I heard a man telling about when he was a boy and about the day he spent with his grandfather. They saw some buzzards overhead and Grandpa suggested that they play a trick on the buzzards. He told the boy to lay down in the field and not to move. If he wanted to go to sleep that would be OK. Then, when the buzzards came down to eat the "dead" boy they would take a picture and then scare the birds away.

This all made me start thinking about buzzards. They really are incredibly interesting creatures! First of all in Missouri we have no buzzards. What we call buzzards are vultures. In most of the state we have only turkey vultures. Along the southern border we also have some black vultures. Some folks call them "prayer birds" because they seem to sit for an hour and say grace before they eat. They may just be watching to be sure the carcass is not actually alive.

These birds keep our planet clean. If not for them we would all have died of botulism long ago. They have a special digestive system which allows them to eat very rotten meat and mix it with gastric juices which kill harmful bacteria and botulism germs. They also have some really interesting adaptive behaviors.

For one thing, they gorge themselves and get so full and so heavy that they cannot fly until they actually digest the food. In the meantime, they are very vulnerable to dogs, coyotes, and other predators. If a predator approaches, the vulture can vomit with the force of a firehouse and direct the rotten acidic mess into the face of the predator. This also makes the vulture lighter so it can now take off and fly.

Another unique behavior keeps them cool. Vultures cannot sweat to cool off so they squirt a combination of defecation and urine onto their legs and feet. The uric acid in this mess kills any germs which they may have picked up from the carcasses which they eat. As the mess evaporates from the legs and feet, it takes away heat and cools the birds. This is why their yellow legs and feet always look gray.

Remember all those cowboy movies where the vultures are circling above waiting for the lost or injured cowboy to die? It never happens. Turkey vultures have a wonderful sense of smell and they only eat something that has been dead for a very long time. They are truly carrion connoisseurs.

I really thought that we had a group of vultures using our barn for a roost. Actually, they are only sitting up on top early in the morning to sun themselves. They also gather on top of the old barn just before they fly off to their well-hidden roosting tree. I wondered why I couldn't find their nests in the barn. Well, it's because they don't build nests. They just lay their eggs next to a stump or a rock.

Oh yes, that boy whose grandfather wanted him to play dead for the vultures – Well, it turned out that Grandpa was just tired of all the boy's questions. He was trying to trick the boy into taking a nap. Come on, Grandpa – Questions are good!

Eighty Eight: Rites of the Seasons

Looking back at our own childhoods, I'm sure that we all have certain things that we remember about the coming of various seasons. As I reminisce about a few, see if they ring any bells. Did you have any yearly rituals which heralded the seasons?

As a child, the beginning of any year was the beginning of the school year. Didn't you love going to the five and dime and buying your supplies? I always wanted a zipper notebook. Of course we needed pencil and paper too. Lots of kids had lunch boxes or lunch buckets and their decorations carried great social status. Since we grew so fast, the new school year often meant a new pair of shoes or boots also. The girls like the pretty stuff but we boys wanted combat boots or something manly.

Again, because of growing, winter usually meant a new pair of gloves. I wore lots of pea coats and other winter ware from the army/navy surplus stores but the gloves were always something new. When I was in the primary grades I usually wanted the jersey cowboy gloves with the big cardboard cuffs and fringe hanging down. There couldn't be anything worse than those but all the boys wanted them. The cuffs caught snow and held it around our wrists and the jersey material got wet quickly and took forever to dry out. It's a wonder we didn't all lose fingers to frostbite.

Spring was by far the best. In the spring we boys could take off those heavy combat boots and start wearing high top sneakers. They were comparatively so light that it really seemed like we could fly. My favorite thing about spring was that I was always allowed to get a new baseball cap. I usually chose cardinal red. Then I would sew a big yellow National Rifle Association patch on the front and it became my hunting hat. Sometimes I would put it on my bedpost at night and have trouble falling asleep just thinking of all the adventure which lay ahead for me and that hat.

Finally summer would arrive and school was out. I would miss a lot of the kids but lots of them I would still be seeing in Little League baseball. None of the girls would be there but I never gave a thought to them at that time anyway. The new uniform meant a new hat but I saved it for games and wore my red hat with the yellow patch for everyday use. We were such a small town that we all seemed to know who was on which team anyway. We didn't need to wear the caps for recognition. In fact, I still remember meeting kids around town and being called by my baseball number, number 14, instead of by my name.

Summer was also the time for riding bikes, building orange crate cars, and as much swimming as possible. My parents were great for allowing us boys to dig in the garden and when we wanted a snack we would just dig up a potato or two, wash them off with a hose, and then chonk 'em like apples. A good drink from the hose would quench our thirsts and give us a cool soaking at the same time.

August was the best time of summer because we still had summer fun and yet, we were just a few weeks or days away from seeing our friends and starting the whole year over again!

Eighty Nine: What Became of Shame?

A parking lot drug deal busted by police – The dealer attempts to escape – He hits a police officer with his car – Other officers shoot to stop the driver/dealer/escapee/perp. The young man dies from gunshot wounds. All this was captured on the parking lot's surveillance camera and broadcast on the evening news.

The next day brought the predictable wailing of the mother and the brothers and sisters. All the stories of what a good boy he was and claims that he never got in trouble before. The accusations that the police were trigger-happy and theories about why the police were so eager to kill "innocent" victims.

Whenever I hear one of these stories, I try to imagine what would happen if this had been my brother or one of my cousins who was shot. I think we would have left town. I believe that the shame of being involved in such a thing would force us to keep a low profile and begin to plan for the next phase of our lives after and away from the shame of such an event.

I'll bet that the majority of Midwesterners agree that forgiveness is one of the highest forms of civilized behavior. However the basic idea of civilization must be remembered also. That involves controlling ourselves and treating others with respect. The flip side of this self-control and respect is shame. We should be ashamed of our un-civilized behavior.

I overheard two boys in my class. One, in a normal-volume voice said, "My dad gets out next week." The boy next to him replied, "My grandpa's in too but he won't be getting out any time soon."

The first boy asked, "Why? What did he do?" The second boy explained, "Mostly he was just coming to visit us. You know, first he got naked and then just started driving. He got in trouble when he got out to pump gas."

Yes, I think it's funny too. What's not funny is that these ten-year-olds say for everyone to hear that their family members have broken some of society's major rules and have had to be removed from civilized people. Their discussion was so matter-of-fact and there was no hint of shame! If they are so accepting of this behavior, what are the chances that they too will be breaking the rules during their lives?

One little boy seemed to do something more outrageous with each day that went by. One day, after the police took him away, a co-worker said, "He just has more options in his life than you or me. We get up and decide what we want for breakfast and what we will wear to work. He can get up and decide whether he will get kicked out of school today, or get arrested, or get in a fight, or do his work, or not, or skip school, or assault some girl."

This person was exactly right. For some people, life has no constraints. If there is no shame, anti-social behavior comes easily and the chances for success are small.

Zouave Re-enactors on Parade

Ninety: Zouaves

When the marines were stationed in the halls of Montezuma it was for a reason. They wore their blue jackets with red-striped pants and those brilliant white hats. Standing there, an elite fighting force in the halls of government, the conquered officials could not ignore them. Those eye-catching uniforms were an early form of "shock and awe."

During the Civil War there were other shockingly-clad bright uniforms whose very existence was meant to intimidate. These soldiers proudly referred to themselves as zouaves. This strange word was from the French word "suave" which we know means sophisticated or debonair. These zouave soldiers were meant to look more sophisticated than anyone they encountered.

Can you imagine being a southern infantryman whose army has turned from winning all of the early battles to loosing regularly because of a lack of supplies? You have been running out of shoes, food, bullets, gunpowder and all of the most basic needs of an army. Then just when you couldn't feel any lower, something happens.

A military unit comes into view. They certainly aren't a part of your pitiful outfit. They don't even look like the boys in blue but that's who they're marching with. There they are, right in the center of the formation with bright red, white, and blue uniforms. The baggy red pants are as full as those of a Turkish sultan. Their little blue waist jackets are covered with wild patterns of roped embroidery and their heads are wrapped in big turbans. They carry the Stars and Stripes but they also carry a green and white flag with a Bardic Harp and a border of shamrocks. The southerners must have wondered, "Are they Americans or some new force thrown at us?"

Well, they were American all right and they were also a new force. Many of the zouave units were made up of newly-arrived Irish immigrants who had two things in common. They wanted to prove themselves worthy of citizenship in their new country and they desperately needed a job. Big strapping Irishmen were gladly welcomed into the armies of both sides.

Did these brilliant uniforms intimidate the confederates? We'll probably never know. What we do know is that the zouave units that sprang from St. Louis are very interesting and shocking to see. The Civil War re-enactors in St. Louis have a zouave unit which is often seen in parades. The next time you see the strange uniforms parading down the street, remember who they represent and why a soldier would dress in such an outlandish way.

Ninety One: Head 'em Up, Move 'em Out

It's the early days of Missouri's statehood and you have cattle to sell. How will you get them to market? Well, that's pretty easy to answer because you've seen so many cowboy movies. Cattle like to stay in a herd so you just drive the herd from where you are to where you want to be. This is exactly what the pioneers in Missouri did. – Sometimes all of the way to a railhead.

There is one big difference between a Missouri cattle drive and a Texas cattle drive though. Missouri is not all grassland. A cattle drive often meant pushing them down dirt roads with forest on both sides. It was very easy for cattle to stray. In some places the woods are still populated with wild cattle.

My great-great-grandfather was known as "Bish Malone the Hogbuyer." His days were sometimes spent going from farm to farm on his way to the stockyards in town and picking up two, or ten, or forty head of hogs at each place and then driving them all to market. For the life of me I can't understand how those old-timers could drive a large group of hogs down those dirt roads and past those forests, then through town to the stockyards. Pigs are very independent creatures! They constantly resist being driven anywhere. Especially in the old days when pigs were not as domesticated as they are now.

Somehow he would end up with hundreds of pigs to sell but many of them must have escaped along the way. I suppose that was just the cost of doing business back then. I know for sure that when pigs are <u>in</u> the wild they <u>become</u> wild. I've seen that. The famous Arkansas Razorbacks are not a myth.

Now try this one on for size. They drove huge flocks of turkeys to market in the very same way. This was done well into the 20th century when trucks became available. There are plenty of pictures around of gigantic flocks of turkeys on the main streets, courthouse squares, and stockyards of various towns.

These were not turkeys like we have today. Today's big white birds bred to provide abundant breast and white meat are too heavy to fly. A hundred years ago the turkeys were still very close to what nature gave us. They were leaner and more independent. The farmers must have clipped one or both of their wings and that would keep them from flying away during the drive. But they were still independent-minded and it must have been a challenge to get those birds to walk those many miles from point A to point B.

One last thought. These drives were necessary for one big reason. There was no refrigeration in those days. There were no refrigerator cars on the trains. There was no way to ship carcasses from place to place. The only alternative was to get live animals all the way from the farm to the packing plant in good condition. That required long walks and careful attention if you were to avoid losing all or part of your herd. It's enough to make you turn to crop farming. Oats don't run away.

Ninety Two: Saint Rose Philippine Duchesne

Did you know that there was a saint from Missouri? There was one – and only one. Just listen to what this woman did with her life.

Born into one of the premier families of France she was best known for being stubborn and determined. Her parents arranged several marriages for her but she refused them all. She said she had promised herself to God. As a teenager she asked to visit a convent and then refused to leave. Finally at 25 she was allowed to join. She lived through the French Revolution and the horrors that followed and then through the ups and downs of Napoleon's reign.

By 1805 she seems to have made her decision to come to America and bring the Gospel to the Indians. In 1818, with the encouragement of Bishop Dubourg of St. Louis, she left for Missouri. She and her sisters came to St. Charles which she described as "the remotest village in the United States." They settled into a one-room shack and established the first convent west of the Mississippi. Following instructions, they established the first free school for girls in the entire United States.

Life was hard for the three nuns in St. Charles. Sister Duchesne wrote to friends in France that water froze in the pail between the creek and the cabin. Food froze on the table. They often had no fire because there were no tools for cutting wood. They decided to move the convent and the school. Just north of St. Louis was Florissant and that place seemed perfect for her Order of the Sacred Heart and there was a larger population for her school.

Thanks to her perseverance, by 1850 the Sisters had opened twelve Sacred Heart schools in the New World. Her mission to America seemed a great success. However, she considered her mission a huge failure. She had never been permitted to minister to the Native Americans. She had so much to share and they were so in need! She found an outlet for her desires by supporting and helping the Jesuit priests who were very much involved in serving the Indians.

Then in 1841, retired and in failing health, she went with the Jesuits and Father De Smet to work at a Pottawattamie village. She was greeted with an enthusiastic welcome and a gift of many human scalps. She couldn't speak their language and it turned out that her best service there would be as a good example. The Indians called her "Woman-who-prays-always."

Her health continued to fail her and, after only one year, she was ordered to return to Florissant.

Back at the convent she wrote, "I feel that I am a worn-out instrument, a useless walking stick that is fit only to be hidden in a dark corner." She chose for herself a tiny closet under a stairway and slept there for her final ten years on earth. Before her death she was able to establish schools for white, black and Indian children. She died in 1852 at age 83. She was the model of humility. She considered her life a series of failures. She achieved an extraordinary amount of good works. Her students would stand nearby to watch her face after communion. It was said to actually glow with light. She was an American Saint.

Ninety Three: Simple Pleasures

A couple of my aunts told me of an experience from their childhood. They described running down the hill to get the cows for milking. They ran so their bare feet would barely touch the frosty grass. Then at the bottom of the hill they would hold their feet up to the sun. The sun's warmth on the soles of their feet was described with real joy.

Have you ever had a simple pleasure that sticks with you through the years? I remember riding a bike on a newly-paved street. It is so smooth that you feel like you might be flying. An entire flock of children zigzagging and swooshing like birds soaring on bicycles is a pleasure that I often recall when the local street department has been at work.

Mansfield, Missouri's Laura Ingalls Wilder was great at finding simple pleasures in all situations. Do you remember how she described walking on the "moonpath" across a frozen lake? How about the time that the cow was grazing on the roof of her family's sod house. It fell through and destroyed the roof. That night many children would have cried themselves to sleep because their home was destroyed and they literally didn't have a roof over their heads. Laura couldn't get over the fact that she had the most beautiful ceiling in the world and it was decorated with thousands of stars.

I think that every so often we need a reminder of how important the simple pleasures are and how we need to appreciate the many simple blessings that we all have. "Mr. Edwards Meets Santa Claus" is a chapter from Laura's Little House on the Prairie and it should be required reading for every family with children. There's nothing religious about that story and even families who are not Christian could benefit from re-focusing on what is really important to real families.

Each December I used to ask my students to try and think of what they liked most about Christmas. Sometimes I would ask them to each tell about one favorite Christmas memory. Either way, it was always a shock to them when I pointed out afterwards what they had told the class. Without fail, each child would describe a play time with cousins, going to distant grandparents, a candlelight service at church, some family tradition, or any number of things having one thing in common.

When I pointed out the common factor, the kids were incredulous. But how could they deny it? From their own mouths had come descriptions of family time and family activities. They were so conditioned to equating Christmas with toys and gifts that they seemed to feel that they had flunked some sort of Christmas test by putting family over presents. It was an eye-opening experience for them and an experience which I anticipated year after year. It was one of my simple pleasures.

This year let's all read Truman Capote's <u>A Christmas Memory</u> and give ourselves the opportunity to recognize and revel in the simple pleasures.

Ninety Four: Be Still and Know

Do you remember seeing "Ma and Pa Kettle in the Ozarks?" We laughed at how the characters laid around and, except for talking, some scenes in that type of hillbilly movie showed almost no action at all. The simple lack of motion was a joke to those of us who were accustomed to a fast-paced life.

On the other hand, how often do we say, "If I only had a few minutes to stop and . . . " You fill in the blank. Some of the old hillbillies would probably get a good laugh at the way we live our lives too. Or maybe they wouldn't think it was so funny.

The Bible tells us in Psalm 46:10. "Be still and know that I am God." For this discussion, let's just take the first part. Be still and know. That makes sense all by itself. If we are ever to understand anything in depth we must take some time and give it some serious contemplative thought.

Yet, quiet time for contemplation is something which we seem never to permit ourselves.

When children are losing control we often tell them to take a time out and think about the situation. What great advice that would be to give ourselves. I marvel at the wisdom in some of the old sayings passed down from country folks. I really believe that the wisdom is a product of long hours behind a plow, driving a tractor, gardening, canning food, or splitting wood. Let's also remember that, in times gone by, people had evenings together without commercial entertainment demanding their attention and dominating their thoughts. Be quiet and know. Be quiet and grow in wisdom.

Have you ever attended a meeting with people you didn't know very well and tried to size them up? There is often someone who sits quietly and doesn't say much. I always have a tendency to think of that person as a listener and a thinker. His or her quiet nature buys some respect. (Especially when compared with the blabbermouth who seems determined to get all the attention and none of the respect.) I think the way we grant consideration to the quiet person is a result of our knowing that quiet, thoughtful people are often wise people.

It's interesting to know that the Psalm quoted above is translated from Hebrew and the word for "be still' is "raphah." It also means slack, or let drop, or be weak, or go limp. Today we might say relax or chill out. It's obvious that even more than two thousand years ago, people needed to be reminded to settle down, relax, stop and think about it.

We sometimes talk about a "mountaintop moment" in which something significant becomes clear to us. We attach the name to it because of the times through history when people have sat alone in a remote place and contemplated their lives. In various ways for various people it is a very religious experience. Things come into perspective when viewed from a distance. This seems to work best in a natural setting but the most important component is that we allow ourselves the opportunity to be still – and know.

Ad for a Carrie and Ida's Sears Home

Ninety Five: Here Comes Our House!

Sisters, Carrie and Ida Holtgreve, were from a German family in Franklin County. The Holtgreve family was best known for its general stores. The sisters worked in a shoe factory. They never had financial problems but they certainly weren't considered to be wealthy. In 1926 these sisters decided to buy a house and they managed to do it. How did they pull off such an accomplishment? Partly because the house was ordered from a Sears and Roebuck catalog. Going this route could shave as much as 2/3 off the price of similar houses. Carrie and Ida paid just under $1000 for their home but nice homes could also be purchased for as little as $370.

Sears sold these do-it-yourself projects during the years of 1908-1940 and during that time they sold over 70,000! In addition to the obvious advantage of savings, these homes had other advantages. For one thing, "red-lining" was a common practice in Missouri and other states. These homes provided a way around the red-lining which kept single women, minorities, and recent immigrants out of many neighborhoods or municipalities. Now wealthy families could afford to have a second home on a river or in the country. These homes were all about opportunity and possibility.

Other advantages included the latest in new and modern features. These included electrical wiring, indoor bathrooms, and central heat through a coal furnace. Asphalt shingles were new and they were available on these Sears homes also. Construction was amazingly easy and was usually accomplished by a group of neighbors and family in an event similar to the old-fashioned barn raising. Everything was included including paint, 72 coat hooks, and even a doorbell. Another advantage was that Sears and Roebuck would guarantee the quality of the product.

Now, there were down sides to these homes also. One was that the 25 tons of materials and 30,000 parts had to be shipped in railroad boxcars. People who did not have a railroad nearby couldn't buy a home. Another disadvantage was that when the material arrived, it had to be picked up and transported to the building site. You couldn't leave it sitting by the tracks and hope to find it all there the next day.

Both of these problems confronted Carrie and Ida because, just as they were waiting to receive their new home by rail, their father died. Now instead of anticipating their new house, they had to plan his funeral. In spite of all that confronted them, they had to spend their time in a cold rain hauling their own 25 tons from the railroad depot to their lot.

Many Missouri towns are close to railroads and probably most of those have Sears homes among the others. They're hard to identify because they were 370 popular designs, they have been modified and modernized over the years, and they have been enlarged. Carrie and Ida's home was purchased by their church after their deaths and torn down to make a new addition. No one seemed to realize that there was a historical significance there. In Missouri, Kirkwood, Webster Groves, and Ferguson seem to have the most of these remaining structures. The St. Louis metro area has over 300.

Ninety Six: Missouri's Day and Symbols

Way back in 1915 the state legislature set aside a special day so that each year we could observe Missouri Day – a day to think about what makes this place special. I find that now most people don't even know what or when Missouri Day is. Well, here's your reminder. The third Wednesday of each October is that day, different from the others.

Part of Missouri day in every school is always a reminder of what our state's official symbols are and why symbols are important to our identity. For instance, the official state seal contains our motto. "SALUS POPULI SUPREMA LEX ESTO." Translated from Latin it means, "The welfare of the people shall be the supreme law." That's a pretty good motto. It has often been used to remind our lawmakers that no law should ever work against the good of the people. Can you say Eminent Domain?

The state flower is an unusual one because it grows on a tree. Sometimes called the red haw or the white haw, it blossoms in beautiful clusters on the hawthorn tree. Our state tree also has attractive flowers. The dogwood is a beautiful sign of spring every year all across the Show Me state.

Lot's of people know that the bluebird is Missouri's official state bird, but that's not exactly right. Our feathered friend is the Eastern Bluebird. Western bluebirds are blue all over. Ours are the little guys with red chests and white trim with blue backs and wings. Red white and blue just like our state flag.

The state nut is the walnut. The husks are used for dye, the nutmeat for food, and the wood for beautiful hardwood furniture. English walnuts are also good for food but they don't do well in most places unless grafted to the roots of our good old black walnuts.

A group of school kids in Lee's Summit convinced the legislature to adopt the crinoid as our official state fossil. This relative of the starfish looks like a plant but it's really an animal that thrived in this place 250 million years ago when this was a vast inland sea.

We have a very appropriate state mineral. When the first settlers came here they were looking for lead. The lead ore which they found is called galena. It's shiny, angular, and very heavy. It's a very interesting mineral. Our state rock is Mozarkite. Its name comes from Missouri, and Ozarks, and the Latin "ite" for rock. It often has bands of pinks, greens, purples, and creamy whites running through it and the Indians used it for arrowheads.

Of course the mule is our state animal. We have an aquatic animal, the paddlefish, and an official fish, the channel catfish. The honeybee is our state's insect and the fiddle is our official musical instrument. That goes well with our official dance, the square dance. There are many more but you'll have to find those yourself on the next Missouri Day.

Ninety Seven: Dowsing

How is it that some of the smartest people I know have come to believe in the practice of finding water, minerals, graves, and other things by a strange, seemingly magical process called divining? Could it be that there is something to the process? As I mentioned, they came to the belief – they didn't start there. Many who were skeptics have changed their minds.

Called dowsing, water witching, and divining, the process always has certain things which are necessary. The "dowser" uses a forked stick, a bowed stick, or two rods held parallel to each other. No one can tell you why it happens but they all agree on how it happens. The universal signal seems to be the rods pulling downward toward the person's feet when they are over the water or other desired object.

The divining rods can be made of several kinds of wood or certain metals. Each dowser has his or her own favorite. There seems to be no difference in abilities when it comes to men or women. Either can be very successful with divining and even children can often do this if they are patient. Everyone develops his or her own style.

We usually hear of divining for water or minerals but there are other options. I manage two historic cemeteries and many of the oldest graves are not marked with stones. Some of the oldest stones are two worn to be read. Therefore, I sometimes encounter people who need help in locating old graves. A few specially trained dogs can do this but a much more common practice is to have diviners walk the area.

In Laclede County Lillian Humphreys has repeatedly demonstrated not only her ability to find underground water but also her ability to tell exactly how far down the well must be dug in order to reach the water.

One common phenomenon is that of the person who cannot get results when trying to dowse. This person then tries again with a successful dowser touching the first person's back or shoulder. All of a sudden, the first person can experience the same success as the real dowser.

Now water can be located with ground penetrating radar and with instruments suspended from airplanes or helicopters. How expensive would that be? Professional well-drillers say that it is fairly common for people to choose the location of a new well and have water witching as a part of the location process. There may be another large percentage of people who consult the dowser before the driller is ever called.

I often read through articles from the past. They explain old-fashioned practices which were common then but which now seem strange or even silly. I would love to be able to read this a hundred years from now and see if divining was still practiced or if it was considered the stuff of witch doctors. My guess is that it will still be used for one reason. It seems to work.

Ninety Eight: Schnitzel Banks

If you know what a schnitzel bank is, you probably live in a German part of the state. Elsewhere it would be called a cobbler's bench, or a carpenter's bench, or a harness-maker's bench. It was one of the most vital tools for folks on the frontier. It was probably used at every homestead in Missouri and may have been the first tool unloaded from every covered wagon. Schnitzel banks are still seen at crafts fares and are used all over the state. Schnitzel bank literally means "carver's bench."

It really is a bench. People sit on them. They straddle the bench and in front of them is the rest of its length. It was always made from a board twelve inches wide and about five feet long. To give strength and support its users, they were about two inches thick. The height of the bench depended on the height of its maker and user. An attachment on the top clamped down and held things in place like a vice. This attachment, called a clamp block, was controlled by either of the person's feet.

A pioneer could use them to hold spokes in place while they were smoothed down with a sharp instrument called a spoke-shave. Strips of wood for baskets are still made by holding sections of oak in place on the schnitzel bank and shaving off thin strips with the draw knife. Hides can be held tight on the schnitzel bank as the harness maker or cobbler cuts the leather. It also holds the leather while it is being joined together or finished. In a time when a person couldn't run to the store for a new handle for the axe, hammer, or shovel, you could just sit down at your bench and make one.

In the old days barrels were the containers used for almost every kind of product, both wet and dry. They could be rolled on their rims by one person so were very practical. The individual curved wooden boards making up the barrels are called staves. If you were to make barrel staves, the schnitzel bank would be the perfect tool. After the barrel was completed, a good cooper would use another kind of schnitzel which we would call a "down-shave." It would be used to smooth the outside of the barrel and give it a smooth finished look.

This most useful of all contraptions got its name from the cutting instruments which were used with the bench. Draw knives and spoke-shaves were among the various cutting tools which the Germans named schnitzels. These are different from other cutting instruments because they are drawn toward the craftsman.

The other popular kind of schnitzel was the champfer-knife. If you ever saw one of these you would remember its "L" shape with one straight handle and one which was set perpendicular to the five inch blade. The champfer-knife was used to trim the tops off the barrel staves and make the assembled barrels even all around the top.

These schnitzel banks are always handmade and have a very primitive look. If you ever see one at a sale or an antique store, latch on to it. You'll not only have a great collector's piece but a true and personal piece of our nation's history.

Ninety Nine: Before Air~Conditioning

What did you do to stay cool in the days before air-conditioning? It's been a while hasn't it? Some younger people have never lived in a time without machines to make our air cool and dry through the hot humid summers. Some of the children in my class really didn't know how to cope with heat.

They were little houseplants who stood around at recess whining at me with statements like, "I'm sweating." They wanted me to do something about their perspiration! These poor little guys lived in air-conditioned homes, rode to school in air-conditioned cars, studied in air-conditioned classrooms, shopped in air-conditioned stores, played in air-conditioned buildings and generally lived air-conditioned lives.

What will we do if someday we have to live without the cost and pollution involved in air-conditioning our environment? Here are some of the things that our forefathers did.

When the first settlers arrived in Missouri they were clever enough to build porches all around their homes. They called the porches "galleries." These French men and women planned ahead so they could always sit and work or relax on these porches and have shade no matter what the time of day.

Both French and British soldiers stationed here wore wool uniforms. Imagine what they went through in coping with the heat and humidity! We have learned to dress appropriately.

American settlers built log cabins and were also clever about that. They would often start with a small and basic log shelter. Later they would add on but without directly adding to the original building. The new addition and the old original structure were sometimes connected with a single roof leaving a breezeway between. These were called dog trot cabins and the breezeway provided a shady place in the day and a covered cool place to sleep at night. Many Americans used to sleep outside in the summer. An awning would keep the dew off the sleepers and everyone seemed to sleep well in the cool night air. Screened porches were tops.

People also had summer kitchens. They cooked in a little kitchen behind the house rather than heat up the family's living quarters. I suppose the barbeque grill serves that same purpose.

People also learned where the coolest places were and would try to spend time there. For instance the basement is the coolest part of the house. Fans pulling that cool air upstairs can help a lot. Theaters and the largest stores might have been "air-cooled." This would usually mean that a big fan in the back room was blowing across ice and pushing the cooled air out into the store or theater. Nature makes some cool places too. I remember the terribly hot summer of 1954 and how, when my father came home from work, a picnic would be ready and we would all go down to the park at Bennett Spring. The spring sent cold water rushing up out of the ground and it actually cooled the entire valley. Wading made it even better.

Acclimation seems to be the main thing however. Those folks were just accustomed to the heat and we aren't. Maybe, as our soldiers return from the Middle East, they can teach us how they cope with 140° plus. It can be done. We should be doing it better.

One Hundred: Sentenced to Sunday School

Even back in the good old days before we were so politically correct and common sense was still considered a virtue, kids could find ways to get in trouble. I remember one of those kids. His name was not Roger, but we'll call him that. Roger was related to a good friend of mine so I had known him for years. He was a likeable kid and always seemed kind of exciting. He was often on the edge of acceptable behavior and was clever and entertaining. To me, he was sort of a Huckleberry Finn.

I don't know what Roger did to find himself before the Judge of the Juvenile Court but there he was. The judge was trying to avoid sending Roger off to a reform school or to seriously stain his record. His solution was to offer Roger a choice. He could spend some time in a juvenile facility or he could spend one full year of regular attendance in Sunday school. Roger opted for Sunday school.

He chose to come to our particular Sunday school and his personality instantly changed our quiet and orderly little group. Our teacher, Mrs. Romans, wasn't one to show her emotions but she must have taken a few steps up the frustration ladder at this time. Roger was, without any doubt, a challenge but she continued on through the curriculum. Even as little kids, we felt sorry for her.

I'll never forget the day that she was teaching us about Christian love. She told us to love our neighbors as ourselves. She told us to love even our enemies! Then Roger made it personal. "Mrs. Romans," he said. "Do you love everybody in the world?"

She thought for just a moment and said, "Sometimes it's hard, but I really try."

Then one of the boys asked, "Mrs. Romans, do you even love Roger?"

She didn't pause a moment. She just smiled and said, "Oh, yes. That's easy." The perfect answer and it came without hesitation, without a second thought, without any gushy stuff to embarrass Roger.

Mrs. Romans taught the perfect lesson that day. She didn't do it with her lesson plan, room preparation, or multi-sensory involvement. She didn't insert cross-curricular activities, or a flowery Christian vocabulary. She just lived the lesson right there in front of us.

I moved on and moved away. I don't know exactly what happened to Mrs. Romans except that she taught many more Sunday school kids before she died. I don't know what happened to Roger either. The last I knew though was that he was staying out of serious trouble and seemed to be an entertaining rascally good kid. I sometimes saw little bits of Roger in other boys later as I spent my thirty years in teaching. They were often my "sparkplugs" who kept class interesting and gave the group its personality. I would hope that if some of them were to get into trouble that some judge might have the courage to consider the possibilities of a good Sunday school class. There are still people like Mrs. Romans waiting for them.